As one of the world's longest established and best known travel brands, Thomas Cook are the experts in travel.

For more than 135 years our guidebooks have unlocked the secrets of destinations around the world, sharing with travellers a wealth of experience and a passion for travel.

Rely on Thomas Cook as your travelling companion on your next trip and benefit from our unique heritage.

Thomas Cook **pocket** guides

ALGARVE

Written by Chris and Melanie Rice, updated by Victoria Trott

Published by Thomas Cook Publishing
A division of Thomas Cook Tour Operations Limited
Company registration no. 3772199 England
The Thomas Cook Business Park, Unit 9, Coningsby Road
Peterborough PE3 8SB, United Kingdom
Email: books@thomascook.com, Tel: + 44 (0) 1733 416477
www.thomascookpublishing.com

Produced by Cambridge Publishing Management Limited
Burr Elm Court, Main Street, Caldecote CB23 7NU

ISBN-13: 978-1-84848-245-6

© 2006, 2008 Thomas Cook Publishing
This third edition © 2010
Text © Thomas Cook Publishing
Maps © Thomas Cook Publishing/PCGraphics (UK) Limited

Series Editor: Adam Royal
Production/DTP: Steven Collins

Printed and bound in Spain by GraphyCems

Front cover photography: © LOOK Die Bidagentur der Fotografen/Alamy

CONTENTS

WHAT'S IN YOUR GUIDEBOOK?

Independent authors Impartial, up-to-date information from our travel experts who meticulously source local knowledge.

Experience Thomas Cook's 165 years in the travel industry and guidebook publishing enriches every word with expertise you can trust.

Travel know-how Thomas Cook has thousands of staff working around the globe, all living and breathing travel.

Editors Travel-publishing professionals, pulling everything together to craft a perfect blend of words, pictures, maps and design.

You, the traveller We deliver a practical, no-nonsense approach to information, geared to how you really use it.

● Azulejo *tiles at Estói Palace*

INTRODUCTION
Getting to know the Algarve

Key:
- ◯ City
- ◯ Large Town
- ◯ Small Town
- Motorway
- Main Road
- Minor Road
- ✈ Airport
- Railway

Atlantic Ocean

Vila Nova de Milfontes
São Luis
N389
Santa Luzia
N120
N263
Garvão
N393
Cavaleiro
Milharadas
Odemira
Aldeia dos Palheiro
São Teotonio
Santa Clara-a-Velha
Barragem de Santa Clara
Carvalhal
Caeiro
Santana da Serra
Odeceixe
Oleiros
Moitinhas
Nave Redonda
Samouqueira
Foz do Arroio
São Marcos de Serra
N266
Ponta da Atalala
Aljezur
Fóia ▲ 902
Monchique
Perna Seca
Arrifana
Marmelete
Caldas de Monchique
Alfambra
Casais
São Bartolomeu de Messines
Bordeira
N268
Corsino
Pereira
Silves
Cumeada
Barragem da Bravura
Carrapateira
N120
Porto de Lagos
Algoz
Bensafrim
IC4
Portimão
Lagoa
Pedralva
Lagos
Alvor
Armação de Pêra
Albufeira
Vila do Bispo
Burgau
Praia da Rocha
Carvoeiro
Cabo de São Vicente
Praia da Luz
Ponta da Piedade
Santa de Rocha
Montechoro / Oura
Zavial
Salema
Sagres
Ponta de Sagres

Algarve
0   10 km
0   5 miles

Atlantic

Getting to know the Algarve

The Algarve is a favourite with tourists seeking warm winter breaks, golfing holidays and family summer holidays. In the west lies a succession of bays, inlets and rocky coves, sheltered by dramatic sandstone cliffs, creating magical places to laze away the day.

The coastline along the central Algarve between Faro and Portimão is full of large hotels, quality resorts, holiday homes, new championship golf courses, restaurants and nightlife. In the east, the long unbroken expanses of golden sand are ideal for swimming and sunbathing. The eastern Algarve is quieter in general but hotels line the long wide beach at Monte Gordo near the Spanish border.

Golfers flock to the Algarve for the 35 or so golf courses there, which vary from beachfront courses with water features to cliff-top courses surrounded by pine trees. There are opportunities for deep-sea fishing, windsurfing, horse riding, sailing, lawn bowling and tennis. And for walkers, there are plenty of dunes and cliff paths that are perfect for a gentle ramble with outstanding views. If you're after a

AZULEJO TILES

Glazed, multicoloured *azulejo* tiles began appearing in the Algarve more than 500 years ago and are now used to decorate everything from park benches to house fronts, restaurants and even train stations. The oldest examples are in churches and chapels, where the predominantly blue tiles usually depict scenes from the Bible.

WHAT IS *FADO*?

Fado music is as important to the Portuguese as *flamenco* is to the Spanish. *Fado* ballads are plaintive and dramatic, usually about lost or unrequited love and the ups-and-downs of life. In Portuguese, they say this is a feeling of *saudade*, or nostalgia. The accompaniment is provided by a *viole* (Spanish guitar) and a *guitarra* (a pear-shaped, 12-string guitar).

⬤ *Nossa Senhora de Guadalupe chapel*

proper hike or mountain bike, you can head into the Serra de Monchique with steep, lush mountain trails and a therapeutic spa at the end of it in the natural springs of Monchique's historic town.

There is plenty of culture and heritage to discover from Silves, the ancient capital of a Moorish province, and Prince Henry the Navigator's school at Sagres to Gothic and Manueline architecture in chapels and churches across the region. Soak up the atmosphere of the historic centres of Faro, Tavira and Castro Marim, buy local ceramics and jewellery, and don't forget to visit one of the gypsy markets for a few bargains to take home.

There's just as much variety in the nightlife: you can dine out at a romantic cliff-top restaurant, on a terrace overlooking the beach or in a converted fisherman's cottage, stop for a sundowner in a cocktail bar on a beach esplanade, or enjoy a pint of beer in an English- or Irish-style pub. For a touch of local colour, sign up for a traditional *fado* evening, on offer at many of the larger resorts, or go to a village restaurant barbecue. If you're still raring to go, dance the night away in a disco or nightclub, or, if you're feeling lucky, have a flutter in one of the casinos.

THE BEST OF THE ALGARVE

There's something for everyone in the Algarve, including families, golf fans, sun worshippers, watersports enthusiasts, fresh-air fiends and party animals. Here's the pick of the crop:

TOP 10 ATTRACTIONS

- **Miles of long golden beaches**, such as the 2 km (1¼ miles) at Falésia (see page 54), or the 20-km (12½-mile) stretch at Monte Gordo (see page 49).

- **Tickle your taste buds**, whether it's a picnic at the 'end of the world' in **Cape St Vincent** (see page 59) or dinner at a sophisticated fish restaurant in **Vilamoura marina** (see page 41).

- **Get away from the crowds** with a countryside excursion to **Monchique** for mountain walks and perhaps a spa at the end of the day (see page 66).

- **Take a day trip** to explore the historic city of **Faro** (see page 75), or consider an overnight stay in the country's capital, **Lisbon** (see page 83).

- **The Algarve is renowned for its golf**, with 35 beautiful and varied courses. The world-class **Vale do Lobo** has a breathtaking backdrop (see page 47).

- **Explore some of the Algarve's past**. The ancient castle at **Silves** is the largest in Portugal and has spectacular views (see page 71).

- **Nightlife** – clubbers should make a beeline for lively **Albufeira** (see page 37).

- **Big-game fishing** – try your hand at hooking a huge shark or marlin (see page 103).

- **Shopping** – pick up some local crafts and jewellery (see page 98), or find a bargain at one of the local markets (see page 96).

- **Theme parks and zoos** – kids (and a few adults) will love the Algarve's theme parks. Check out **Zoomarine**'s dolphin shows, aquarium and pool (see page 36) or have a day of fun at **Slide & Splash** (see page 31).

Praia da Marinha beach at Armação de Pêra

SYMBOLS KEY

The following symbols are used throughout this book:

ⓐ address **ⓣ** telephone **ⓕ** fax **ⓦ** website address **ⓔ** email
ⓛ opening times **ⓘ** important

The following symbols are used on the maps:

𝒊	information office	○	city
✉	post office	○	large town
▣	shopping	○	small town
✈	airport	◼	POI (point of interest)
✚	hospital	▬	motorway
♖	police station	―	main road
▣	bus station	―	minor road
◈	railway station	―	railway
✝	church	**Ⓜ**	metro

❶ numbers denote featured cafés, restaurants & evening venues

---

RESTAURANT CATEGORIES

The symbol after the name of each restaurant listed in this guide indicates the price of a typical three-course meal without drinks for one person.

£ = under €20   ££ = €20–€30   £££ = over €30

▶ *Coves at Lagos beach*

RESORTS
Places under the sun

Salema & Burgau

Typical red-roofed fishermen's houses, a small sandy beach and cobbled streets rising gently up sandstone cliffs characterise the villages of both Salema (pronounced 'Sah-lay-mah') and Burgau (pronounced 'Bur-gow'). With just a handful of shops, bars and restaurants, holidaymakers come here to enjoy the peace and quiet as well as the stunning scenery of northwestern Algarve.

Life in these tiny communities revolves around the harbours, where the local fishermen mend their nets and wash out the squid pots. Boat trips head along the coast from Salema harbour to the rocky crevices of **Ponta da Piedade** where egrets nest or, in the opposite direction, where swimmers can enjoy a dip before sitting down to a barbecue on a secluded beach. The beauty of the area can also be appreciated on foot by following the two-hour switchback walk over the headlands between Burgau and Salema, which takes in the remote coves of **Ponta da Almadena** and **Boca do Rio**.

Wake up in time to watch the sun rising over the bay and you will see the fishermen hauling in the first catch of the day; alternatively, you can enjoy their harvest at lunchtime by sampling octopus, sardines or white sea bream in a harbour restaurant.

SHOPPING

There is a newsagent, a supermarket and a souvenir shop on Rua 25 de Abril in Burgau.

Salema has a couple of supermarkets as well as handicraft and souvenir shops on the waterfront. At **Loja do Tosca** you will find top-quality one-off designer Portuguese and ethnic clothing and accessories (beautiful belts and shoes). Sculptures are also for sale.
❸ Rua dos Pescadores, Salema ⏰ 09.00–late

The nearest banks and pharmacies are in Praia da Luz but there is an ATM in the square in Salema. For more comprehensive shopping, head for Lagos.

THINGS TO SEE & DO

Birdwatching
Full- and half-day trips, led by an expert, can be booked through the tourist office at Portimão. **()** 282 41 91 32

Burgau Sports Centre
The facilities here include a gym, football, basketball, tennis and squash courts, swimming pool and aerobics sessions, plus a children's playground and children's sports mornings. **()** Rua Vale de Burgau **()** 282 69 73 50 **()** www.algarvesports.com

Parque da Floresta Golf and Leisure Resort
The excellent Parque da Floresta club offers lawn bowling (**()** 10.00–dusk; competitions Mon), an 18-hole golf course plus golf academy, four tennis courts, a fitness and leisure centre, mountain-bike rental, kids' club, spa and walking tours. **()** Vale do Poço, Budens **()** 282 69 00 13 **()** www.parquedafloresta.com

⬤ *Salema's beach*

TAKING A BREAK

Salema

Boia Bar £ A popular place with the young crowd, it serves full English breakfasts, tea and toast, and sandwiches and salads at lunchtime. It has a verandah overlooking the sea and an all-day bar. ⓐ Rua dos Pescadores 4 ⓣ 282 69 53 82 ⓛ 10.00–23.00 daily

Restaurante Barraca £–££ This well-established restaurant, just a few metres from the beach, specialises in *cataplana* (fish stew) (see page 90) and *arroz de tamboril* (monkfish rice). ⓐ Largo dos Pescadores 2 ⓣ 282 69 77 48 ⓛ 12.00–15.30 & 19.00–22.00 Wed–Mon

Mira Mar ££ Good food is available all day at reasonable prices in this typical Algarve restaurant. Try the *cataplana*. ⓐ Travessa Miramar 6 ⓣ 919 56 03 39 ⓛ 12.30–23.00; closed Sat

Burgau

Beach Bar ££ Not only the perfect location, sitting on a raised terrace above Burgau beach, but good food – from full meals (lobster salad and T-bone steaks are the specialities) to simple burgers. ⓐ Main beach ⓣ 282 69 75 53 ⓛ 09.30–02.00, restaurant open 12.00–15.00 & 19.00–22.00; restaurant closed Mon but bar open

Casa Grande £££ Charming old manor house with its former winery is now a restaurant serving up a varied menu that alternates daily between Portuguese and Italian, with a good choice for vegetarians and delicious desserts. Occasional live music and folk dancing. ⓐ Road to Praia da Luz ⓣ 282 69 74 16 ⓛ 19.00–23.00 daily (Mar–Oct)

Praia da Luz

In the past decade or so, Praia da Luz (often just called Luz, pronounced 'Loosh') has grown into a popular resort but the whitewashed villas and holiday apartments still blend harmoniously with the picturesque old houses clustered around the old fishing harbour. Its blue-flag beach and soft sand edged by great slabs of smooth rocks make it great for sunbathing and the bay's sheltered waters make it ideal for water-skiing, windsurfing, sailing and diving. Luz has its several local shops, bars, restaurants and a disco near the waterfront.

Luz's attractive hinterland is ideal for walks and drives. Take the path from the car park at the eastern end of the village to the top of the headland, where an *atalaia* (obelisk) stands at a height of 108 m (360 ft) above sea level. From here there are coastal views as far as Sagres.

The gently rolling hills to the north of Luz are best explored by car. The road winds through a landscape dotted with farms, ancient wells, fig trees and quaint villages like Barão de São João.

THINGS TO SEE & DO

Beach Hut Watersports Centre

From dolphin tours to bananas and from kayaking to surfing, there's something for all ages here.

ⓐ Beachfront (look for the flags) ☎ 919 55 34 76 🕐 10.00–17.00 daily (May–Oct)

> **SHOPPING**
> The **Centro Comercial** on the seafront has a number of outlets selling clothes, food, magazines and groceries. **Baptista's** supermarket is in the centre of the village. Situated below the Dolphin restaurant is the colourful **Africa Craft Shop**, specialising in curios and handicrafts from Southern Africa. ⓐ Rua da Calheta 🕐 14.00–21.00 daily

◆ *Watersports at Praia da Luz*

Chico Water Sports Offers everything from windsurfing and sea kayaking to banana boats and pedaloes.

ⓐ Beachfront, Praia da Luz ☏ 965 60 53 79 ◷ 09.00–19.30 daily (May–Oct)

Fortaleza da Luz

Luz's 16th-century fortress has been beautifully restored to house a fine restaurant (see page 20) and exotic gardens. Even if you don't intend eating here, don't be shy to ask to look in.

ⓐ Rua da Igreja 1 ☏ 282 78 99 26 ⓦ www.fortalezadaluz.com

Horse riding

Tiffany's Riding Centre caters for young and old, novices and experts alike. Offers lessons from one hour to a whole holiday course.

ⓐ Vale Grifo, Almádena ☏ 282 69 73 95 ⓦ www.teamtiffanys.com
◷ 09.00–13.00 & 15.00–19.00 daily

Parish church

Situated near the waterfront of the old village, the picturesque parish church has a Mass on Sundays at 09.00, medieval vaults and a gilded baroque altar.

ⓐ Largo da Igreja

Sports

Facilities at the **Luz Bay** and **Ocean** clubs include swimming pools, saunas, a Turkish bath, gym, mini-golf, tennis and squash courts.

TAKING A BREAK

Bar Habana £–££ Whatever it is, they have it at this all-day-all-night meeting spot on the beach, known locally as 'The International'. All-day breakfast at all hours, with burgers, curry, Chinese favourites, ice cream and an extensive cocktail list. Bar Habana is also where Luz's webcam is situated.

ⓐ Beachfront ● 09.00–02.00 daily

Paraiso £–££ Right on the beach, this light and airy bar-restaurant is a good choice for seafood, snacks, drinks and great views on the terrace.

ⓐ Beachfront ● 282 78 82 46 ● 10.00–20.00 daily

Royal Garden £–££ A popular Chinese restaurant with seafood specialities and clay-pot casseroles with a choice of duck, chicken, beef or pork. Also does a takeaway service. ⓐ Rua 25 de Abril, Loja A ● 282 76 72 39 ● 12.00–15.00 & 17.30–23.00 daily

Atlantico ££ A modern Portuguese restaurant specialising in grilled meat and fish, washed down with local wines. Vegetarian 'daily special'.

ⓐ Avenida dos Pescadores (opposite Fortaleza da Luz) ● 282 78 87 99 ● 19.00–22.00 Tues–Sun, closed Mon ● www.atlanticoluz.com ● Booking recommended

Bar Carib ££ A restaurant serving three meals daily, with a swimming pool and tennis court (rackets and balls for hire). The special barbecue (Sun lunchtime and Wed evening) is a bargain, but book ahead. Sandwiches and children's meals also available. ⓐ Montinhos da Luz, 1 km (½ mile) from Praia da Luz ⓣ 282 78 89 08 ⓛ 10.00–late; closed in winter

Fortaleza da Luz ££ This terrace restaurant serves modern international cooking, including inventive pizzas, lots of vegetarian choices and great cakes during the day. Wonderful views of the rocky beach below. ⓐ Rua da Igreja ⓣ 282 78 99 26 ⓛ 11.00–15.00 & 18.00–24.00 daily ⓦ www.fortalezadaluz.com

Maharaja da Luz ££ Restaurant serving up good northern-Indian food with a takeaway service. ⓐ Centro Comercial, Edificio Luz Tur (above the pharmacy) ⓣ 282 78 95 79 ⓛ 12.00–14.30 & 18.00–24.00 daily

O Cangalho ££–£££ Portuguese cuisine served in a traditional farmhouse setting. Home-baked bread, roast suckling pig and chicken *cabidela* (stewed in a rich sauce with rice) are among the specialities here. ⓐ Quinta Figueiras, Sítio do Madronhal, Brão de São João ⓣ 282 68 72 18 ⓛ 12.30–15.00 & 18.30–22.00 Tues–Sun, closed Mon

AFTER DARK

Duke of Holland £–££ English-run bar and restaurant offering all kinds of food, from snacks to full meals. Steaks in sauces are their speciality. Quiz and karaoke nights and a large-screen TV showing major sports events. ⓐ Rua da Praia 19 ⓣ 282 78 98 88 ⓛ 11.00–02.00 Tues–Sun, closed Mon

Le Privé Club serving up a mix of Portuguese and English pop music, especially popular with the younger crowd. ⓐ Rua José da Conceição Conde, beneath Centro Comercial Via Sul ⓛ 23.00–04.00 daily

Praia da Rocha

Located just outside Portimão, Praia da Rocha is now one of the Algarve's 'veteran' resorts, having been one of the first to commercialise at the beginning of the 1960s. Known as one of the main party places in the region, apart from Albufeira, and one of its busiest resorts during the summer months, there's still plenty of space on its beaches for sunbathers. Its name literally means 'rocky beach', due to the spectacular red and yellow sandstone outcrops on the seafront. At one end of Rocha's beach, a tunnel has been carved in the rocks to give access to the bays beyond, and to the east there is a modern marina that has led to the building of new hotels, apartments, restaurants and bars there.

THINGS TO SEE & DO

Beaches and new marina
As well as the main sandy beach at Praia da Rocha, which is 100 m (110 yds) wide, there is easy access to Praia do Vau, west towards Alvor, and at the eastern end there's another small beach beside the marina,

● *See where the 'beach of the rocks' got its name*

built in the last few years. There are several restaurants and bars around here, and it's a prime spot to relax while listening to the comforting 'clank clank' of the yachts moored there.

Fortaleza da Santa Caterina

This fortress dating from 1691 offers spectacular views at sunset – beach and ocean on one side, marina on the other. Inside there's a chapel dedicated to St Catherine of Alexandria, and below there is a small garden, with beach views.
ⓐ Avenida Tomás Cabreira ⓛ Daily ⓘ Free admission

Portitours

This company offers jeep safaris in 4x4s into the heart of the Algarve, as well as boat trips along the coast. In addition they organise coach, walking, bike and canoeing trips with experienced guides.
ⓐ Edificio Portimar, Alto do Quintão, Portimão ⓣ 282 47 00 63
ⓦ www.portitours.pt

Rocha Express

Also called 'funny train', this tourist train leaves the Miradouro every 30 minutes, calling at Fortaleza and Praia do Vau. Tickets can be bought on board.
ⓛ 10.00–12.00 & 16.00–23.30 daily

SHOPPING

There are two supermarkets, **Alisuper** and **Himalaia**, on Avenida Tomás Cabreira. There is a **gypsy market** on the road to Portimão (close to Club Praia da Rocha) on the first Monday of each month. Look along side streets and in some of the larger hotels for local crafts, souvenir shops and individual boutiques, or for more choice head into Portimão, especially around Rua Comerciale. Look out for copper and tin items as well as lace, baskets, footwear and painted textiles.

Watersports

Water-skiing and pedalo rental (including snorkels) are all available from the beach. Praia da Rocha also has excellent conditions for windsurfing – boards can be rented by the hour, with lessons for beginners.

TAKING A BREAK

Pizzeria La Dolce Vita £ This pasta and pizza restaurant has more than two dozen pizza varieties to choose from. Look out for bargain lunch specials and their Italian ice cream. ⓐ Avenida Tomás Cabreira, opposite the Hotel Algarve Casino ⓣ 282 41 94 44 ⓛ 12.00–15.00 & 18.30–23.00 daily

Salsada do Zé £ Wonderfully located on the beach, this is a great place to enjoy breakfast, lunch or dinner. From sandwiches to kebabs and from veggie dishes to traditional Algarve fare, there's something for everyone here. ⓐ Beach, Praia da Rocha (walk down steps by Hotel Jupiter) ⓣ 967 25 51 82 ⓛ 09.00–late daily

Casalinho ££ It may not look much, but this place has a loyal army of fans who come here for top-quality Portuguese/international cooking with flambé specials. ⓐ Main beach, below the Penguin terrace ⓣ 282 42 25 79 ⓛ 09.30–24.00 daily

Chang Thai Restaurant ££ Authentic Thai restaurant with a wide-ranging menu and options for the kids. There's Thai dancing, and the owners offer massages too (not in the same room!). ⓐ Edificio Rio a Vista, Rua Antonio Feu ⓣ 282 42 79 08 ⓛ 12.00–15.00 & 18.00–24.00 daily

Barrote £££ Upmarket restaurant in a 4-star hotel by the beach. Known for its meat dishes, the *barroso* beef with oven-baked potatoes is particularly good. ⓐ Hotel Jupiter, Avenida Tomás Cabreira ⓣ 282 41 50 41 ⓛ 12.00–15.00 & 19.00–22.00 daily

Titanic £££ Dress up for a special evening out at this relaxing flambé and fish restaurant, with a wide choice of international dishes. ⓐ Rua Eng Francisco Bivar ⓣ 282 42 23 71 ⓛ 18.30–23.00 daily

The Village Inn £££ Owned by Canadian Cathy Lancaster, this friendly restaurant seats around 30. The menu is 'everyday food' with plenty for vegetarians. ⓐ Mexilhoeira da Carregação, about 2 km (1¼ miles) east of Portimão, on the other bank of the River Arade ⓣ 282 41 20 36 ⓛ 18.30–22.00 Tues–Sat, closed Sun & Mon ⓘ Reservations recommended

AFTER DARK

Casino American roulette, French roulette, blackjack, punto e banco and 306 slot machines will relieve you of your euros here. Dinner is served at 20.30 nightly, followed by a Las Vegas-style show at 22.30. ⓐ Hotel Algarve, Avenida Tomás Cabreira ⓣ 282 35 73 81 ⓛ 16.00–04.00 daily ⓘ Passport required

Farmer's Pub Established in 1980, this is the place to come for a fun night out or to watch a match on TV. There's live music most nights in summer. ⓐ Rua Antonio Fell ⓣ 282 42 57 20 ⓛ 10.00–04.00 daily

Katedral Located on Rocha's main party street just back from the beach, this is a large nightclub with bars, satellite TV, pool tables and disco featuring several different music styles. ⓐ Avenida Tomás Cabreira ⓣ 282 42 43 36 ⓛ 23.00–07.30 daily

On the Rocks This continues to be Praia da Rocha's trendiest cocktail bar and club, with a terrace overlooking the beach. ⓐ Avenida Tomás Cabreira ⓛ 10.00–04.00, happy hour 10.00–20.30 daily

Armação de Pêra

Palm trees shade the promenade at Armação de Pêra (pronounced 'Armasow de Perra'), a modern resort boasting one of the longest expanses of sand in the Algarve. In fact, it stretches all the way to Galé, a satellite of Albufeira.

To the east of the resort is Praia dos Pescadores where, early in the morning, small colourful boats depart, as they have done for centuries, in search of the day's catch. Get here at about 10.00 to see them return with their booty. The old part of town lies in the cobbled streets behind the beach, and here you'll find many of the local bars and fish restaurants. To the west of the resort are the Algarve's classic rock stacks and cliffs topped with white villas. Boat trips from the beach pass these on their way to the spectacular stacks and caves between here and Carvoeiro (see page 30).

THINGS TO SEE & DO

Alcantarilha parish church

Inside Alcantarilha the macabre chapel is lined with human skulls and bones – the remains of some 1,500 parishioners, permanently exhibited as a cheerful reminder of human mortality!

SHOPPING

The huge **AlgarveShopping** centre is located in Guia on the N125 towards Albufeira. It has a Continente hypermarket, plus a large range of national and international fashion stores from Accessorize to Zara. If you're after something local and handmade, head inland from Armação de Pêra to Porches, which is renowned for its pottery (see page 97). See the potters at work before buying from one of the outlets selling the ceramics along the EN125 highway.

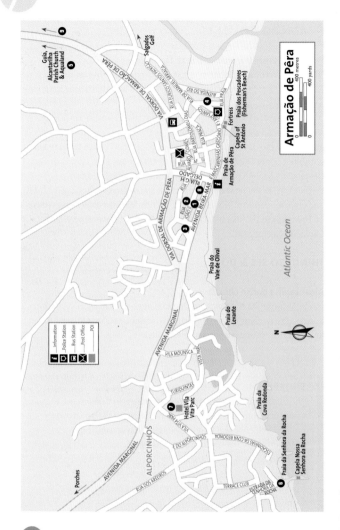

Armação de Pêra

Information
Police Station
Bus Station
Post Office
POI

Atlantic Ocean

Guia,
Alcantarilha
Parish Church
& Aqualand

Salgados
Golf

Praia dos Pescadores
(Fisherman's Beach)

Fortress
Capela of
St António

Capela de
Armação de Pêra

Praia do
Vale de Olival

Praia do
Levante

Praia da
Cova Redonda

Hotel Vila
Vila Parc

Praia da Senhora da Rocha

Capela Nossa
Senhora da Rocha

Porches

ALPORCINHOS

N

0   400 metres
0   400 yards

⬥ *Fresh fish, straight from the sea, to boat, to restaurant*

Aqualand

Portugal's largest water park offers aquatic rides and amusements in a garden setting. Not just for kids, there is entertainment for all the family.

ⓐ Alcantarilha ① 282 32 02 30 Ⓦ www.aqualand.pt

Golf

Located on the flatter ground behind Praia de Galé, **Salgados Golf Course** is a links-style 18-hole course of 6,080 m (over 6,650 yds). Handicap certificate required. Courses available.

ⓐ Vale de Parra ① 289 58 30 30

Ⓦ www.algarvegolf.net/courses/salgados.htm

Nossa Senhora da Rocha

'Our Lady of the Rock' is a sailor's chapel, dating back to the 16th century, perched on a spectacular headland approximately 3 km (2 miles) west of the resort. If you make the effort to climb up to the chapel, the interior contains some lovely *azulejos* (tiles) and votive model-ship offerings (check opening times first with the tourist office in Armação de Pêra). A rock-cut tunnel gives access to the lovely beach of Senhora da Rocha.

ⓐ Estrada da Nossa Senhora da Rocha, Praia da Senhora da Rocha (3 km/2 miles) west of Armação da Pêra, overlooking the sea)

Wine tasting

The Vila Vita Parc hotel has its own wine cellars (*cave de vinhos*) and offers wine-tasting tours. You can choose from Portuguese, port and Vila Vita wine tours, depending on your taste and how much you want to spend. Decorated with tiles from Egypt, Australia and Greece, the cellars are ample with 11,000 bottles of wine stored here at any one time.

ⓐ Hotel Vila Vita Parc, Alporcinhos, Porches ⓣ 289 31 01 00
ⓦ www.vilavitaparc.com

TAKING A BREAK

O Pai Pinguim £ ❶   A promenade café selling ice creams, crêpes, sandwiches and other snacks. ⓐ Avenida Beira-Mar

Pizzeria Italiana Lóasi £ ❷   Cheap and cheerful pizzeria for when you want a simple but satisfying snack. ⓐ Edifício Atlantico 4, Rua do João II
ⓣ 282 31 28 69

O Fernando ££ ❸   Excellent fish dishes are served in this typical Portuguese restaurant. Try the grilled fresh salmon. ⓐ Rua Rosa dos Ventos 10 ⓣ 282 31 34 81 ⓛ 10.00–24.00 daily

A Grelha ££ ❹ It claims to be the oldest traditional restaurant in the Algarve – it's certainly one of the best for fresh fish and seafood, though it also offers a good selection of meat dishes. ⓐ Rua do Alentejo 2 ❶ 282 31 22 45 🕓 12.00–15.00 & 18.00–22.00/22.30 daily

Marisqueira Hera ££ ❺ You'll see live fish in the tanks at this Algarvian seafood restaurant. Specialities include monkfish rice, seafood platter and *cataplana*. ⓐ Largo Infante Dom Henrique 2 ❶ 282 31 27 70 🕓 12.00–24.00 Fri–Wed

Villa d'Italia ££ ❻ Formerly at Hotel Pestana Porches Praia, this well-known Italian restaurant has moved just over the road to the Algar Club. Good value for money. ⓐ Algar Club, Senhora da Rocha (opposite Viking Hotel) ❶ 282 31 70 77 🕓 12.30–15.00 & 18.30–22.30 daily

The Ocean £££ ❼ As the name suggests, this restaurant has great sea views but you'll need to dig deep and dress up, so save this one for that special night out. Located in the 5-star deluxe Vila Vita Parc hotel complex, this is a fine-dining restaurant with a choice selection of wines from the cellar. Reservations required. ⓐ Hotel Vila Vita Parc, Alporchinhos ❶ 282 31 01 00 🕓 17.30–22.00 ⓦ www.vilavitaparc.com ❗ Reservations from 19.00; last seating 20.30

AFTER DARK

Beachcomber ❽ This bar is popular with the party crowd, with two rooms of dance music and cocktails to cool you off. ⓐ Avenida Beira-Mar, Lote 13 ❶ 282 31 30 91 🕓 22.00–02.00 daily

Calixto ❾ One for the party-goers, this two-floor disco-club plays salsa and chart music, has ladies' nights and foam parties. ⓐ Beco das Palmeiras ❶ 967 46 37 47 🕓 23.00–06.00 daily (Mar–Oct)

Carvoeiro

Armação de Pêra's smaller neighbour, Carvoeiro (pronounced 'Carvo-aero') is highly photogenic, with brightly painted fishing boats and spruced-up, whitewashed villas. Reached by a long and narrow valley road, which eventually ends in a pocket-handkerchief of golden sand, Carvoeiro is one of the prettiest resorts in the Algarve.

BEACHES

This stretch of coast is characterised by its rocky promontories and sandstone cliffs. The beach at Carvoeiro itself is quite small and crowded so it's worth exploring down the coast. The gentle shelving beach at **Centianes**, 2 km (1.2 miles) east of Carvoeiro, is good for surfing. At one point the only way you could get to it was via a set of steps but there's now a pathway. Further east, this is still the only way to get down to **Praia do Carvalho**, also known as Smuggler's Cove due to the caves and nooks. Continue on to **Praia de Benagil** for boat rides along the coast, and **Praia da Marinha** for pristine sands, archways and rock stacks in the

◆ Centianes beach, near Carvoeiro

sea. To the west of Carvoeiro, **Carneiros** and **Pintadinho** are moderate-sized beaches each with a café, and **Ferrugado** is popular with surfers.

THINGS TO SEE & DO

Diver's Cove is a registered PADI dive centre based in Carvoeiro and offers lessons for all levels up to divemaster. They organise boat, shore, night, freshwater, wreck and cave dives. They also have a two-person apartment available to rent, with a garden and pool.

ⓐ Quinta do Paraiso ⓣ 282 35 65 94 ⓦ www.diverscove.de/dive-uk.htm. There's also a dive school within the Tivoli Almansor.

ⓣ 282 35 11 94 ⓦ www.tivoli-diving.com

Slide & Splash

Whirlpools and waterslides, including the new 'Black Hole', are among the features of this popular fun park. Facilities include shops, bars and a restaurant. Slide & Splash runs a bus service with pick-up points all along the coast (ask the tourist office for further details).

ⓐ Vale de Deus, Estombar ⓣ 282 34 08 00 ⓦ www.slidesplash.com
ⓛ 10.00–18.00 daily ⓘ Admission charge

Tennis

The **Performance Tennis School** is located within the Carvoeiro Club de Ténis and offers courses in a friendly environment with multilingual

SHOPPING

A Praça Velha, 'the old market', deals mostly in mass-produced pottery, though there are other handicrafts and souvenirs for sale.

ⓐ Rua dos Pescadores ⓛ Daily

For better quality pottery go to **Porches** (see pages 25 and 97). The nearest real market is at **Lagoa** (second Sunday of each month).

Also on the main EN125 at Lagoa is **Mundo do Sapato** (Shoe World), with some bargain brand-name footwear.

teachers. As well as nine hard courts, there are two Canadian-clay, one artificial-grass and two practice-wall courts.

ⓐ Carvoeiro Club de Ténis ① 282 35 78 47 Ⓦ www.tenniscarvoeiro.com

Wine tasting

Lagoa is famous for rough red wines with a high alcohol content. **The Lagoa Wine Co-operative**, on the Portimão road, opens its cellars for conducted tours and wine tastings.

① 282 34 21 81 Ⓛ Usually 10.00–12.00 & 14.00–18.00, but call to check
ⓘ It is advisable to book at least 24 hours in advance

TAKING A BREAK

A Boa Vida £–££ This café-cum-restaurant has Brazilian specialities such as *muqeca* (stew) of prawns, *pincanha* (Brazilian-style grilled meats, black

GOLF

Vale de Milho Designed by four-time Ryder Cup player Dave Thomas, architect of the Belfry Brabazon Course in Warwickshire, England, this is an attractive course and surprisingly challenging for every golfer. Water hazards play a part in 4 of the 9 holes on the par-30 course. Ideal for practising your short game and excellent value for money. ① 282 35 85 02 Ⓦ www.valedemilhogolf.com. The **Pestana Golf Resort** has four courses. The **Gramacho** is an 18-hole, 72-par course with 27 varied greens, designed by former world no.1 player Nick Price and golf-course architect Ronald Fream. **Silves Golf**, which has spectacular views, encourages and rewards attacking play. **Beloura**, designed by Rocky Roquemore, offers 18 holes at the foot of the Serra de Sintra. The 71-par, 18-hole **Vale da Pinta**, also created by Fream, is a championship course with rolling terrain – definitely one for the experienced golfers. The **Pestana Academy** is also based here, along with its practice areas, shop, restaurant and bar. ① 282 34 09 00 Ⓦ www.pestanagolf.com

beans and garnishes) plus tropical fruits for dessert. ⓐ Estrada do Farol 21 ⓣ 282 35 41 69 ⓦ www.algarve-restaurants.com/aboavida ⓛ 16.00–23.00 daily

Primavera £–££ Mediterranean dishes, more than half of which are Italian inspired, fill the menu of this bright, attractive restaurant. In the summer steaks and pasta are served in a shaded beer garden. ⓐ Rua das Flores 2 ⓣ 282 35 83 42 ⓦ www.restaurante-primavera.com ⓛ 18.30–late Thur–Tues, closed Wed

Bon Bon Restaurant ££ Located to the west of Carvoeiro in the village of Sesmarias, this comfortable restaurant has an international menu from medallion of beef to Oriental-style chicken and vegetarian options. Reservations required. ⓐ Cabeço das Pias, Sesmarias ⓣ 282 34 14 96 ⓦ www.algarve-restaurants.com/bonbon ⓛ From 19.00 Tues–Sun, closed Mon ⓘ No credit cards

Restaurant L'Orange ££ Newly refurbished restaurant with a pretty terrace. Portuguese-style grilled fish and meat dishes are on the menu along with curry and vegetarian options. ⓐ Mato Serrão ⓣ 282 35 72 97 ⓦ www.algarve-restaurants.com/orange ⓛ 18.30–22.00 Mon–Sat, closed Sun ⓘ No credit cards

AFTER DARK

Bar Havana A cosy cocktail bar with a Latin tinge, expect Cuban music and Latin-American cuisine. ⓐ Estrada do Faro ⓣ 969 76 99 56 ⓛ 18.30–late; 2 for 1 cocktails until 8pm

O Bote A genuine veteran on the club scene, this disco remains popular for its themed party nights and terrace where you can cool off. ⓐ Largo da Praia ⓣ 282 35 72 85 ⓦ www.botedanceclub.com ⓛ 23.00–06.00 Tues–Sat, closed Sun & Mon

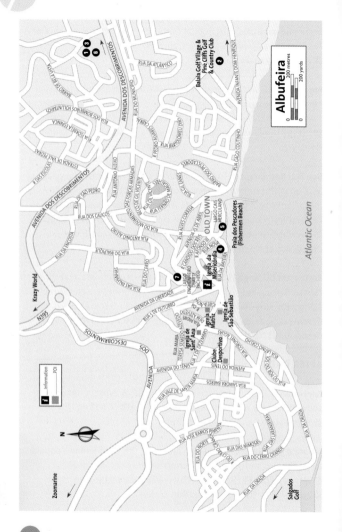

Albufeira

Albufeira

One of the liveliest resorts in the Algarve, Albufeira (pronounced 'Ahl-boo-fair-a') was called 'castle on the sea' by the Moors. The charm of the original fishing village has been preserved in the twists and turns of cobbled lanes, lined with pretty, whitewashed houses.

BEACHES

At the **Praia dos Pescadores** ('fishermen's beach'), local fishermen unload their catch, mend their nets and occasionally touch up the paintwork on their boats. There are fish auctions here, daily, from 08.00 to 10.00 hours. The main town beach, approached by a tunnel cut through the rock, is excellent for swimming and sunbathing but tends to become crowded. To the west are the smaller beaches of São Rafael, Coelha and Castelo.

THINGS TO SEE & DO

Diving
PADI-certified **Indigo Divers** offers lessons for beginners as well as more challenging trips for experienced divers.
🕿 289 58 70 13 🆆 www.indigo-divers.pt. Another choice is **Easy Divers**
🕿 966 19 22 99 🆆 www.easydivers.pt

Krazy World
Once called Krazy Golf, this theme park has evolved into Krazy World featuring Amazonia, a zoo featuring pythons, alligators, turtles and exotic birds, a petting farm with llamas, ponies and camels, plus mini-golf, a pool and restaurant. There are live animal shows and pony rides during the summer months.
🄰 Lagoa de Viseu, Algoz, 30 minutes from Albufeira by car or bus
🕿 282 57 41 34 🕒 10.00–18.00 Wed–Sun Oct–June; 10.00–19.30 daily (July–Aug)

Zoomarine

This large theme park has live shows featuring dolphins, sea lions, tropical birds and birds of prey. There's also an aquarium, marine birds, an exhibition centre and high-definition cinema plus a conservation programme that rehabilitates many marine species back into the wild. Alongside the zoo, there are fun rides, pools and green spaces where you can picnic.

ⓐ Estrada Nacional, Guia, 10 km (6 miles) from Albufeira
Ⓦ www.zoomarine.com Ⓛ Times vary

> ### GOLF
> There are three main courses near Albufeira. **Herdade dos Salgados** is a renowned 18-hole, 72-par course with several lakes and close proximity to the sea. It also has a driving range, golf school and pro shop. Ⓣ 289 58 30 30 Ⓦ www.salgadosgolf.com. At **Pine Cliffs Golf & Country Club**, the golf course is part of a self-contained holiday complex. At 9 holes it is smaller but set in beautiful grounds surrounded by pine trees with sea views, plus you have the added benefit of other sports and leisure facilities onsite. Ⓦ www.pinecliffs.com. **Balaia Golf Village** is also a complex and has a popular 9-hole course. Ⓦ www.balaiagolfvillage.pt

TAKING A BREAK

The heart of the town's nightlife is the pedestrianised square of **Largo Enghenheiro Duarte Pacheco**, lined with restaurants and bars. On summer nights there is a carnival atmosphere here, with stalls lit by fairy lights selling arts, crafts and souvenirs, and crowds of visitors thronging the narrow alleyways.

Great India Tandoori £–££ ❶ Small but popular Indian restaurant with a wide choice of tandoori, balti and karahi dishes. ⓐ Areias de São João
Ⓣ 289 58 77 33 Ⓛ 11.30–15.30 & 18.00–23.00 daily

Johnny Hooper's Saxophone Bistro ££ ❷ Opened in 2006, saxophonist Johnny Hooper plays live at this restaurant-bar every Tuesday and Friday at 20.30 and the menu is mainly Mediterranean. ⓐ Rua Almeida Garret ❶ 963 17 66 35 ⓦ www.johnnyhooper.com ❷ 18.00–01.00; dinner served until 22.00 (22.30 Tues & Fri show nights); Sun lunch 12.00–16.00 with Brazilian band on terrace 14.00

O Licorne ££–£££ ❸ The food at this restaurant is excellent, with an atmosphere and plush décor to match. Tables are well spaced in front of a hearty fireplace. Vegetarian dishes are always available. ⓐ Estrada de Albufeira, between Albufeira and Olhos d'Agua ❶ 917 31 32 07 ❷ From 18.30 Mon–Sat, closed Sun

Aldar £££ ❹ Superb Moroccan cuisine at this restaurant in the Sheraton Algarve with dishes such as lamb couscous and tagine tfaya with chicken and olives. Make sure you book ahead. ⓐ Sheraton Algarve, Praia de Falesia ❶ 289 50 01 00 ❷ 19.00–22.30 Tues–Sat, closed Sun & Mon

A Ruina £££ ❺ This is perhaps Albufeira's most famous restaurant, a labyrinth of ancient rooms serving top-quality fish and shellfish. There is also a terrace overlooking Fishermen's Beach. ⓐ Rua Cais Herculano ❶ 289 51 20 94 ⓦ www.restaurante-ruina.com ❷ 12.30–15.00 & 19.00–23.00 daily

AFTER DARK

Diamond Sports and Karaoke Bar ❻ Catch Premier League football live at this sports bar on one of several large-screen TVs. There's also karaoke here most evenings. ⓐ Rua Alexandre Herculano 33 ❶ 289 54 29 52 ⓦ www.diamondsbar.com

Kadoc ❼ Open during the summer months at the weekends, this large nightclub has five floors of party music with resident DJs and guests. ⓐ Estrada de Vilamoura ❶ 289 36 04 85 ⓦ www.kadoc.pt (site in Portuguese) ⓔ kadoc@kadoc.pt

Vilamoura

Vilamoura covers a wide area of hotels, holiday villas and golf complexes, but the focal point is its marina, around which every conceivable amenity can be found. One of the most popular resorts in the Algarve, you can expect to spot the rich and famous here, even the odd Premiership footballer or two. Low-rise hotels painted in pastel shades, broad, tree-lined avenues and tastefully landscaped parks lead up to the marina.

The marina at Vilamoura is the largest in Portugal, with berths for up to 1,500 yachts. Boats leave from the quayside to explore the fascinating Algarvian coastline, with its myriad coves, beaches and unusual rock formations – some yachts will take you as far as Portimão and back. Big-game fishing (blue shark, tuna and record-breaking black marlin) is also popular, while the watersports on offer include scuba diving, water-skiing and windsurfing. The marina is a place for people-watching, window shopping or promenading, especially at night when the entire

⬥ The marina – Vilamoura's focal point

harbour is illuminated. Souvenir outlets and chic boutiques alternate with smartly turned out cafés and terrace restaurants, offering everything from pizzas and pancakes to chow mein and chicken *piri-piri*. Karaoke is a popular form of entertainment in the family-friendly bars, which stay open well into the small hours.

THINGS TO SEE & DO

Cerro da Vila
Vilamoura means 'Moorish village', but the town's origins date back to Roman times. A new museum has been built around the remains, which include a villa, a farm and baths, and displays the coins, mosaics and other artefacts found here from the 1st to 3rd centuries AD.
ⓐ Avenida Cerro da Vila ⓣ 289 31 21 53 ⓞ 09.30–12.30 & 14.00–17.00 daily (Nov–Apr); 09.30–12.30 & 14.00–18.00 daily (May–Oct)
ⓘ Admission charge

GOLF
Vilamoura is one of the best located resorts in the Algarve for golfing with easy access to some of the best courses in the region. There are six actually in Vilamoura with another half a dozen at Almancil. The **Old Course**, as the name suggests, is the oldest of the resort's golf courses but remains popular and challenging with its setting of narrow fairways and pine trees. **Laguna Golf Course** has wider fairways but the marshy ground and bunkers provide their own challenges. **Millennium Golf Course** has a mixture of open ground, narrow fairways and pine trees, while the **Victoria Clube de Golf** is a new championship course set in wetlands and carob, olive and almond trees, so expect plenty of water features. **Pinhal Golf Course** is also set among pines, with views of the sea and small greens. ⓦ www.algarvegolf.net. Finally, **Vila Sol Spa & Golf Resort** is a mature course with pine, fig and oak woodland, with plenty of lakes and bunkers. ⓦ www.vilasol.pt

Roma Golf Park If you're not quite up to the Old Course at Vilamoura, try this excellent little crazy golf course themed to the Roman finds next door at the Cerro da Vila museum. Two lots of 18 holes are surrounded by fountains and pools.

📞 289 30 08 00 🌐 www.romagolfpark.com 🕐 10.00–18.00 daily

Health and fitness

Brown's This state-of-the-art sports centre has a full-size grass pitch, gym, astroturf pitch, cross-country track, sand pitch, three tennis courts, indoor and outdoor pools as well as a Turkish bath and a bar. ⓐ Caminho dos Golfes 📞 289 32 27 40 🌐 www.browns-club.com 🕐 08.00–22.30 daily

Tennis

Vilamoura Ténis Centre offers lessons and 12 courts for hire (five floodlit). 📞 289 32 41 23 🌐 www.premier-sports.org

Watersports

With the marina being such a focal point in Vilamoura, watersports are high on the agenda for visitors. **Polvo Watersports Algarve**, based at the marina, offers boat charters, dolphin-watching cruises, parascending, jet-ski hire, wakeboarding, water-skiing and banana rides. ⓐ Marina Vilamoura 📞 289 30 18 84 🌐 www.marina-sports.com

TAKING A BREAK

Don Alfonso £–££ Popular with locals and tourists, favourite desserts include the homemade *crêpe suzette*, mango pudding and cheesecake. ⓐ Patios da Marina 📞 289 31 26 88 🌐 www.donalfonso-restaurant.com 🕐 18.00–23.30 daily

Maharaja ££ One of the oldest Indian restaurants in the Algarve, with various regional specialities from tandoori to biryanis. ⓐ Avenida da Marina, Aparthotel Olympus 📞 289 38 88 94 🕐 12.30–15.00 & 18.30–23.30 daily (May–Oct)

Mama Putih ££ Indonesian restaurant richly decorated with paintings and woodcarvings, and a mouth-watering menu of spicy meats, fish and vegetable dishes. ⓐ no. 112, Fonte de Boliqueme ❶ 289 36 02 97 ❶ 18.30–22.30 Mon–Sat, closed Sun

Rei dos Mares ££ A small restaurant with a terrace and nautical décor, located on Vilamoura marina. The menu includes a mixture of Portuguese and international dishes including fresh fish, *cataplana* and peppered steaks. ⓐ Marina Plaza ❶ 289 31 51 62 ❶ 15.30–23.00 daily

Willie's Restaurant £££ Michelin-star chef Willie serves up international-influenced cuisine such as seafood ravioli in vermouth cream and pan-fried monkfish on mustard crème sauce with potato mousse. You definitely need to book ahead for this one. ⓐ Rua do Brasil 2 ❶ 289 38 08 49 ⓦ www.willies-restaurante.com ❶ 19.00–22.00 Thur–Tues (Mar–Dec)

AFTER DARK

Casino Vilamoura As well as having gaming rooms with a range of table games, including Portuguese dice, blackjack, American roulette and poker, **Casino Vilamoura** has around 500 machines such as roulettes, kenos, poker and slots. Outside of the gambling area, there's entertainment with live shows and dinner, restaurants, bars and a disco. ⓐ From the EN125 at the crossroads to Quarteira, follow signs to the casino. ❶ 289 310 000 ⓦ www.solverde.pt ❶ Restaurant 20.30–01.00; Black Jack Disco 23.30–06.00 Thur–Sat; slots 16.00–04.00; gaming rooms 21.30–04.00; closed 24–25 Dec ❶ Passport required

Irish & Co Part of a chain of Irish bars in Portugal, this bar-restaurant serves traditional Irish food and drinks, and has regular live music. ⓐ Centro Comercial, Marina Vilamoura ❶ 289 38 01 54 ❶ 11.00–02.00 daily

Quarteira

Once a typical Algarvian fishing village, Quarteira (pronounced 'Kwar-tay-rah') has become a fully fledged seaside resort that complements its more hip neighbour, Vilamoura, but it is not for those seeking a lively nightlife. There are miles of golden sand stretching, almost without interruption, to Vilamoura in one direction and Vale do Lobo in the other, lined with white hotel blocks and apartments. The shops are concentrated around Avenida Dr Francisco Sá Carneiro, as are the many restaurants and bars specialising in such succulent seafood dishes as *cataplana*. Fishing is still a way of life here: the auctioneers sell off the day's catches in the fish market to the west of the beach. Watersports, golfing, tennis and other leisure amenities are all within easy reach of the resort.

THINGS TO SEE & DO

Aqua Show Family Park A water park with rollercoasters, slides, wave pool, swimming pool, whirlpool, sky-dive show and parrot show. There's also a museum here that tells the history of Portugal through various historical personalities. ⓐ Semino EN396 ❶ 289 38 93 96 ⓦ www.aquashowpark.com ❶ 10.00–18.30 daily (June–July & 1–15 Sept); 10.00–19.00 (Aug)

> ### SHOPPING
> Quarteira's **market** (held every Wednesday) on the east side of the town is one of the largest and most colourful in the region. Fruit and vegetables are the mainstay, but you'll also find clothes, towels, tablecloths and souvenirs, often at bargain prices – try bartering here. For more conventional shopping, head for the pedestrianised precinct leading into Rua Vasco da Gama.

Horse riding

Quinta dos Amigos, a farm just outside Quarteira, has a riding centre with qualified, English-speaking instructors. Riding lessons are available as well as organised rides into the countryside and along the beach. Facilities also include two swimming pools, one for children.

① 289 39 33 99 **Ⓦ** www.equus-algarve.com

BEACHES

Quarteira's long, sandy blue-flag beach stretches virtually uninterrupted all the way to Faro. It has excellent bathing conditions. Artificial sea defences keep the water calm for swimming, and the beach is well provided with sun loungers, umbrellas, windbreak screens and pedalos. A leisurely stroll along the promenade is the best introduction to the beach area, with its varied selection of waterfront bars and restaurants.

⬤ *Quarteira's beach*

TAKING A BREAK

Cantinho do Norte £–££ The daily specials are excellent value at this rustic restaurant specialising in the cuisine of northern Portugal. Specialities include baked kid and codfish from the north and *cataplana* and seafood rice from the local area. ⓐ Quatro Eastadas ⓣ 289 39 73 21 ⓛ 11.30–15.00 & 18.00–23.00 daily

Girafas £–££ This pizzeria on the beachfront also does good hamburgers and Brazilian food. Somewhere to take the kids. ⓐ Edificio Atlantido II, Avenida Infante Sangres ⓣ 289 30 20 22 ⓛ 12.00–15.00 & 19.00–22.00 daily

A Pizza da Villa £–££ A real taste of Italy on the Algarve, with pizzas and pasta dishes served in a checked-tablecloth ambiance, or to take away. ⓐ Off Avenida Marginal ⓣ 289 31 57 70 ⓛ 10.00–23.00 daily

Rei do Churrasco £–££ Charcoal-grilled chicken, ribs, chops and steaks are the speciality at this light and airy restaurant, with a good selection of Portuguese wines and a takeaway service. ⓐ Rua 25 de Abril 30 ⓣ 289 31 30 81 ⓛ 12.00–15.00 (except Mon & Wed) & 19.00–23.00 daily

AFTER DARK

Bar Sete This is a popular and busy bar situated right on the marina attracting celebs, sports celebs and their fans. It also has a restaurant. ⓐ The Marina ⓣ 289 31 39 43 ⓛ 09.00–02.00 daily

Black Jack Disco Open all year, this is the Casino Vilamoura's own night-club with four bars (see page 41 for information on the casino). Dress to impress. ⓐ Casino Vilamoura, Quarteira ⓣ 289 31 00 00 ⓦ www.blackjackdisco.com ⓛ 23.30–06.00 Thur–Sat

Vale do Lobo & Quinta do Lago

Vale do Lobo (pronounced 'Val doh Lobo') and Quinta do Lago (pronounced 'Keenta doh Lahgo', meaning 'lake side') are two of the Algarve's most exclusive and prestigious resorts. Here, among pine forests and salt-water lakes, are the villas of Portugal's rich and famous, as well as four championship golf courses, miles of golden sand, some of the best sports facilities in the Algarve and a good selection of bars, restaurants and nightclubs.

The watersports centre at Quinta do Lago offers pedalos, kayaks, canoes and rowing boats as well as water-skiing. Experts are on hand for lessons in windsurfing and sailing. If none of these appeal, you can always join one of the fishing trips on the lakes.

THINGS TO SEE & DO

Capela São Lourenço dos Matos (the Church of Saint Lawrence of The Woods), just outside Almancil (inland a little, northeast of Quinta do Lago), is one of the few to survive the 1755 earthquake. It is decorated from floor to ceiling with the magnificent blue-glazed tiles known as *azulejos* (see page 9). The church is kept locked, but a caretaker lives next door and will open it up for you between the hours of 09.00 and 18.00 (please note that it is not possible to view the church between 13.00–14.30).

Fitness
Facilities at **Barringtons** include a golf academy with floodlit driving range and instruction, squash courts, cricket nets, a fitness centre, sauna and whirlpool. ⓐ Vale do Lobo ⓣ 289 35 19 40 ⓦ www.barringtons.pt

Horse riding
Centro Hípico Pinetrees Approved by the Association of British Riding Schools (ABRS), this riding school is British-run and gives classes for all ages and abilities. They supply all the kit you need, run nature and barbecue rides, and offer a special holiday discount card bought in

45

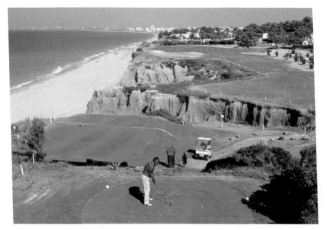

⬤ *Vale do Lobo golf course*

advance. There is also some accommodation onsite and a nearby villa.
ⓐ Casa dos Pinheiros, Estrada do Anção, Almancil ☎ 289 39 43 69
Ⓦ www.pinetreesridingcentre.com ⌚ Horses work from 08.00–11.30 &
16.30–20.00 Tues–Sun; horses rest Mon

Karting

The **Almancil Karting Circuit** was inaugurated by the late great Ayrton
Senna and is a replica of the Jacaregaguá Formula 1 circuit in Brazil.
Independent circuit suitable for children aged four and over.
ⓐ Almancil ☎ 289 39 98 99 Ⓦ www.kartingalgarve.com ⌚ 15.00–18.00
Tues, 10.00–18.00 Wed–Sun & bank-holidays (Feb–May & Oct–Dec);
10.00–20.00 (June & Sept); 10.00–24.00 (July & Aug)

Tennis

The **Vale do Lobo Tennis Academy** has 14 hard courts, a clubhouse, pro
shop and a range of courses all year. ⓐ Vale do Lobo ☎ 289 357 850

GOLF

Pinheiros Altos The first half of the par-72 course is set in woodland, while the second presents some water hazards. ☎ 289 35 99 10

Quinta do Lago Designed by Henry Cotton, the two 18-hole, par-72 courses feature lakes and challenging bunkers. ☎ 289 39 07 00

San Lorenzo A par-72 course exclusively for the use of guests at the Dona Filipa hotel and is one of the finest in Europe.
☎ 289 39 65 22

Vale do Lobo Two challenging and scenic 18-hole golf courses, the Royal, with cliff-top views of the Atlantic, and the Ocean, located alongside a nature reserve on the beach. There's also a golf academy here (see fitness on page 104). ☎ 289 35 35 35

Watersports

The Watersports Centre at Quinta do Lago organises a whole range of activities and courses on both the lake and the sea including sailing, windsurfing, canoeing, jet-skiing, water-skiing and parasailing.
ⓐ Quinta do Lago ☎ 289 394 929 🕘 09.00–19.00 daily

TAKING A BREAK

Cervejaria Marisqueira Central ££ Relaxed seafood restaurant with fresh (and live) fish. Specialities include grilled prawns, seafood *cataplana* and seafood rice. ⓐ Rua Vasco da Gama 88 ☎ 289 31 22 30
🕘 11.00–24.00 daily

O Limoeiro ££ The Lemon Tree, as it's known in English, deftly combines a traditional Portuguese and British menu. ⓐ Avenida Duarte Pacheco 210
☎ 289 39 53 99 🕘 12.00–14.00 & 18.30–late Mon–Sat, closed Sun

Julia's ££–£££ The best place for beach-side drinks and dining, Julia's is renowned for its excellent seafood and secret-recipe African rice.

ⓐ Praia do Garrão (on the beach) ☏ 289 39 65 12
Ⓦ www.julias-algarve.com ⏱ 12.00–24.00 daily

Alphonso's £££ Professional service and a wide selection of excellent food on the menu make this a place for special occasions. The terrace is very pleasant. ⓐ Rua Albertura Mar ☏ 289 31 46 14 ⏱ 12.00–15.00 & 18.30–22.30 Sun–Fri, closed Sat

La Place £££ Elegant French restaurant with sea views and set 'taster' menu options. ⓐ Praça Vale do Lobo ☏ 289 35 33 56 ⏱ 19.00–23.00 daily

Restaurant Vincent £££ Chef Vincent Nas works wonders at this upmarket gourmet restaurant. You'll need to book ahead to guarantee a table but it's worth it to try the menu of internationally inspired cuisine. ⓐ Estrada Almancil, Vale do Lobo ☏ 289 39 90 93 ⏱ 19.00–22.30 Mon–Sat, closed Sun

Restaurante São Gabriel £££ Located between Vale do Lobo and Quinta do Lago, this classy restaurant serves up Mediterranean and international dishes created by chef Torsten Schulz. Reservations required. ⓐ Estrada Vale do Lobo ☏ 289 39 45 21 Ⓦ www.sao-gabriel.com ⏱ 19.00–24.00 Tues–Sun (Mar–Oct)

Teahouse Oriental £££ This pan-Asian fusion restaurant serves cuisine from China to Vietnam and Indonesia and has a good selection of wines. ⓐ Praia Vale de Lobo ☏ 289 35 34 38 ⏱ 19.00–24.00 Sat–Thur, closed Fri

SHOPPING

In **Almancil**, look out for the regular **markets** by the school. Both Quinta do Lago and Vale do Lobo have **upmarket boutiques** and there are golf pro shops at all the main golf courses. For a larger range of international stores, you'll need to drive or take a bus to **AlgarveShopping** at Guia, near Albufeira.

Monte Gordo

People think 'big' in Monte Gordo: the beach is vast, the hotels and apartments are in high-rise blocks, and – for the big spenders visiting the town – there is a casino on the promenade. Popular with Spanish families, who cross the border to enjoy the lower prices, Monte Gordo is a lively resort with clubs, karaoke bars and restaurants offering folk dancing and *fado* evenings.

The main reason for coming to Monte Gordo has to be the beach – 20 km (12½ miles) of shimmering sand, backed by pine forests and citrus orchards, and stretching as far as Praia Verde. Alagoa and Manta Rota's deeper waters are ideal for deep-sea fishing. For watersports enthusiasts, the offshore lagoons are perfect for sailing, water-skiing and windsurfing, while the sea-water temperatures here are the highest in Portugal.

THINGS TO SEE & DO

Boat trips and jeep safaris

Riosul run cruises along the Guadiana river between Portugal and Spain, as well as jeep safaris and a combination of both. They also run a Copper Trail tour, which explores rugged trails to see ancient Moorish mines.
ⓐ Rua Tristão Vaz Teixeira 15c ⓣ 281 51 02 00 ⓦ www.riosultravel.com

Castro Marim

The historic town of Castro Marim is just 7 km (4¼ miles) north of Monte Gordo. As well as having a golf course here, there are a few attractions worth visiting if you want to get away from the beach for a while. The headquarters of the Order of Christ (which replaced the Knights Templar in Portugal in the 13th century) were here before being moved to Tomar. Explore the historic centre, and look out for the Paris Church, the Santo António Hermitage on the hill (with some interesting 17th-century wall panels) and the Castle, which has its origins in the 13th century.

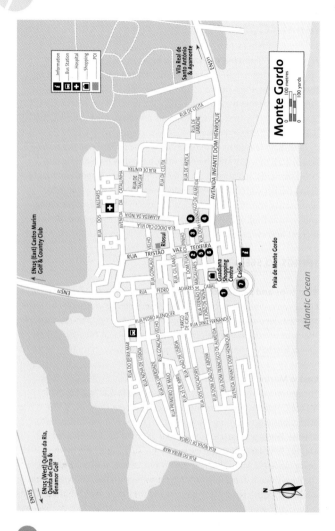

Monte Gordo

Information
Bus Station
Hospital
Shopping
POI

0   100 metres
0   100 yards

EN125 (East) Castro Marim
Golf & Country Club

EN125 (West) Quinta da Ria,
Quinta de Cima &
Benamor Golf

EN125

Vila Real de
Santo António
& Ayamonte

EN511

RUA DE CELTA
RUA DE LARACHE
RUA DE ARZILA
RUA DE CELTA
RUA DE TÁNGER
RUA DE KÉNITRA

AVENIDA INFANTE DOM HENRIQUE

AVENIDA DA CATALUNHA
RUA DOS BALEARES
AVENIDA DA INDIA
ALAMEDA DA INDIA
RUA DIOGO CÃO VILA
RUA FRANCISCO DE ALMEIDA

Riosul
RUA TRISTÃO VAZ VELHO
RUA GONÇALO
RUA GIANNES
RUA DOM ELIAS SOLINHO
RUA DE MACALHÃES
RUA PEDRO ÁLVARES CABRAL
RUA FERNÃO DE MAGALHÃES
RUA JOÃO DE NOVA

Guadiana
Shopping
Centre

Casino

TEIXEIRA

Praia de Monte Gordo

Atlantic Ocean

RUA DO BEIRA MAR
RUA NOVA DE LISBOA
RUA DA LIBERDADE
RUA PRIMERO DE MAIO
RUA TRÊS DE ABRIL
RUA JOÃO DE LISBOA
LARGO DE IGREJA
RUA PEDRO ALENQUER
RUA GONÇALO VELHO
RUA DOS PESCADORES
RUA DOM JOÃO DE NORM
RUA DOM FRANCISCO DE ALMEIDA
AVENIDA INFANTE DOM HENRIQUE
RUA DINIZ FERNANDES
RUA NOVA DE LISBOA
RUA DO BEIRA MAR

N

Cycling

Explore the town and local area by bicycle. You can rent bikes from
Fernandos at daily or weekly rates.

ⓐ Guadiana Shopping Centre, Avenida Infante Dom Henrique
ⓘ 281 51 38 81

Golf

Although you'll have to travel a little further for golf courses than in the
Central Algarve area, there are still opportunities within easy reach.
Castro Marim Golf & Country Club is just 5 km (3 miles) from Monte
Gordo, a luxury development with an 18-hole golf course and another on
the way, as well as apartments and other sports.
ⓘ 281 51 03 30 ⓦ www.castromarimgolfe.com
Quinta da Ria is located approximately 45 km (28 miles) west of Monte
Gordo in the Ria Formosa Natural Park – a flat course with views over the
sea, and which leads to the 18 holes of the **Quinta de Cima** via a local
road. This is a varied course with lakes and a river, plus mountain views.
ⓘ 281 95 05 80 ⓦ www.quintadariagolf.com
Benamor Golf is a little further west (around 16 km/10 miles from
Monte Gordo), a short distance from the historic town of Tavira, and has
an elevated position, looking over towards the mountains and sea.
ⓘ 281 32 08 80 ⓦ www.golfbenamor.com

Shopping

The shops in the Guadiana Shopping Centre and on Avenida Infante
Dom Henrique in Monte Gordo cater for most visitors' needs.

Vila Real de Santo António

The stately 18th-century town of **Vila Real de Santo António**, only
3 km (2 miles) away, makes a pleasant change from sea and sand. It was
laid out on a grid plan by the Marquês de Pombal, famous for redesigning
Lisbon after the Great Earthquake of 1755. Most visitors stop for lunch
(shellfish is the local speciality) before making the short border crossing
to Spain. The road bridge linking Vila Real de Santo António to its Spanish

counterpart, **Ayamonte**, was completed in 1991. Alternatively, you can make the journey by ferry. There are crossings at 40-minute intervals.

TAKING A BREAK

O Dourado ££ ❶ This restaurant, with a shady beach terrace, offers a wide range of traditional Portuguese dishes. Its speciality is a whole range of *cataplana*. ⓐ Avenida Infante Dom Henrique 9 ❶ 281 51 22 02 🕔 12.00–16.00 & 18.30–22.30 Tues–Sun, closed Mon

Rendezvous £ ❷ Diners eat to the accompaniment of pop or *fado* music in this friendly Anglo-Portuguese bar-restaurant. Dishes include favourites such as vegetable or steak pie with chips, chicken *piri-piri* and lasagne. ⓐ Rua Tristão Vaz Teixeira ❶ 281 54 25 69 🕔 10.00–23.00 daily

Snack Bar O Frango Hot £ ❸ Plain or spicy chicken straight from the grill are the specialities of this snack bar. Eat in or take away. ⓐ Rua Diogo Cão Vila ❶ 281 51 27 76 🕔 12.00–15.00 & 18.00–23.00 daily

Goa ££ ❹ An Indian restaurant with a difference. For the uninitiated, a supplementary menu explains the ingredients that provide the distinctive Goan taste. ⓐ Rua Fernando Pó ❶ 281 51 26 06 🕔 11.30–15.00 & 17.30–24.00 daily

Pizzeria Italia ££ ❺ A busy Italian restaurant in the centre of town, offering excellent salads and pasta dishes as well the usual variety of pizzas. ⓐ Rua Tristão Vaz Teixeira ❶ 281 54 28 65 🕔 12.00–15.00 & 18.00–24.00 Wed–Mon, closed Tues

Restaurante O Tapas ££ ❻ With Spain just across the border this tapas restaurant is always a popular choice. Grilled fish is a speciality. Reservations required, especially for large groups. ⓐ Rua Pêro Vaz de Caminha 24a ❶ 281 54 18 47 🕔 12.00–15.00 & 19.00–23.30 Fri–Wed

AFTER DARK

Casino de Monte Gordo ❼ Modern casino with gaming rooms, floor show and restaurant. ❸ Vila Real St Antonio ❶ 281 53 08 00
❶ 16.00–04.00 June–Sept; 15.00–03.00 Mon–Sat, closed Sun (Oct–May)

Nox Bar ❽ Trendy party bar with DJs playing clubbing tunes until the early hours. ❸ Rua Dom Francisco de Almeida 6 ❶ 281 54 39 77
❶ 23.00–06.00 daily

▲ A glimpse of Monte Gordo's beach

Montechoro & 'the Strip'

The inexorable spread upwards and outwards of what was originally the small fishing village of Albufeira has spawned the satellite resorts of what has been christened Nova Albufeira (New Albufeira).

Just a couple of kilometres ($1^1/_4$ miles) east of Albufeira Old Town, perched on the top of a hill, stands the resort of Montechoro, dominated by the landmark Hotel Montechoro. From here, the long, straight Avenida Sá Carneiro (known to everyone as 'the Strip'), lined with bars, restaurants and souvenir shops, descends all the way to the lovely, if often crowded, beach of Praia da Oura. At the crossroads, around halfway down the Strip, the area's name changes from Montechoro to Areais de São João.

BEACHES

East of **Praia da Oura** are the small beaches of **Balaia** and the charming beach cove of **Olhos d'Agua** (literally 'Eyes of Water'), so named for its rock formations. **Açoteias** is a small pine-shaded village next to the splendid golden 2-km ($1^1/_4$-mile) long beach of **Praia da Falésia**, backed by the easternmost cliffs in the Algarve.

⬤ *Hotel Montechoro is a landmark building*

THINGS TO SEE & DO

Albufeira Walk into Albufeira along the cliffs from Praia da Oura. It's a lovely scenic walk. Time it to arrive at sunset, then you can enjoy the pretty sight of Albufeira's fairy-lit central market stalls.

TAKING A BREAK

Senhor Frog's £ Good cheap option for pizzas and pasta.
ⓐ Avenida Francisco Sá Carneiro ⓣ 289 51 46 12
ⓛ 11.30–02.00 daily (Mar–Oct)

Tom & Jerrie's Diner £ If you're in dire need of a good breakfast or brunch after a night on the town, this is the place to come. This is a good family option with roasts on Sundays and good meals for vegetarians.
ⓐ Just off the beach end of the Strip ⓛ 09.30–22.00 daily

The Cottage Restaurant £–££ Tuck into some delicious homemade favourites such as pies, quiches, lasagne, fish and chips, gammon, Sunday roasts and apple crumble for pudding. They serve breakfasts during peak season and half portions are available for most main meals. ⓐ Avenida Sá Carneiro ⓣ 289 54 21 00 ⓦ www.the-cottage.biz ⓛ 09.30–13.30 & 17.30–22.30 daily (mid-Mar–Oct); 18.00–21.30 (Nov–Dec)

SHOPPING

If you are self-catering, there's the **Marrachino** supermarket at the crossroads on 'the Strip', but for more choice go to the large **Modelo** supermarket on the main road to Albufeira. For local colour, continue on the same road to Albufeira's fruit, vegetable and fish market (mornings only). At **Hampers** you can pick up Dutch and English goods including bacon and confectionery or you can catch a bus to **AlgarveShopping** in Guia.

O Poente ££ Smart, traditional restaurant. Grills are the speciality.
ⓐ Brejos-Montechoro, 1 km (¾ mile) behind Hotel Montechoro on road to N125 (by Repsol garage) ⓣ 289 54 14 19 ⓛ 12.00–15.00 & 19.00–22.30 Mon–Sat, closed Sun

The Sizzling Stone ££ Not far from the beach, this is the place to go to cook your own steak or chicken on the hot stone in front of you.
ⓐ Rua Victoria 4, Areias de São João ⓣ 289 51 57 89
ⓦ http://sizzlingstone.com ⓛ 18.30–23.00 daily

AFTER DARK

Erin's Isle Popular Irish bar and restaurant with live music in the beer garden and air-conditioned bar. ⓐ Montechoro Parque, the Strip ⓣ 289 54 29 49 ⓛ 10.00–02.30 daily ⓘ 20.30–00.30 Kids' play area in season

Kiss Disco The Algarve's most famous and buzzing disco with regular theme nights. Entrance charge includes one free drink. ⓐ Rua Vasco da Gama, the Strip ⓛ 23.00–06.00 daily

Mustang Lively and cheap, playing garage and R 'n' B music, this is for the clubbers. ⓐ Areias de São João ⓣ 968 06 86 26 ⓛ 20.00–04.00 daily (Apr–Sept)

MONTECHORO PARQUE
Next to the Hotel Montechoro, this buzzing courtyard comprises several eating and drinking establishments. These include **Puccini's**, **Erin's Isle** (see above) and **Father Ed's**. There's also mini-golf and a bouncy castle.

ⓞ *City walls in Lagos*

 EXCURSIONS
Out & about

◉ *Dramatic cliffs at Cape St Vincent*

Sagres & Cape St Vincent

The small fishing port of Sagres (pronounced 'Sah-gresh') lies just a few kilometres from Cabo de São Vicente, where the fierce westerly winds sweep in from the Atlantic, sending the sea crashing against the rocks. It's an area of stunning natural beauty, with pristine, surf-washed beaches backed by towering cliffs and dunes. Apart from watersports, visitors can look forward to bracing coastal walks, fishing trips, boat trips and jeep safaris.

Standing on Sagres Point, a bleak promontory to the west of the town, is the *fortaleza* (fortress). It was built in the 15th century and its forbidding grey walls once contained Henry the Navigator's famous school of seamanship. From here there are several ways to reach the Cape: by boat (cruises leave from the fishing harbour), by car (via the EN268) or on foot – the cliff-top walk is exhilarating, with fabulous views along the coast and out to sea, particularly at sunset.

On the way is another fortress, the 17th-century Fortaleza do Beliche, restored in the 1960s. Cape St Vincent, mainland Europe's most south-westerly point, was 'the end of the world' until Vasco da Gama, Magellan and other Portuguese explorers opened up the maritime routes to Africa, Asia and the Americas. From the top of the lighthouse it's a 60-m (200-ft) drop to the hazardous rocks below. With good reason, the souvenir stalls at the Cape do a brisk trade in chunky, hand-knitted fishermen's sweaters.

BEACHES

There are four good beaches near Sagres. The largest and most sheltered is **Praia do Martinhal**, near **Baleeira** and the Windsurfing Club. Closer to the village is **Praia da Mareta. Praia do Tonel** is good for surfing, while **Praia do Beliche** is an excellent sandy beach, but is vulnerable to strong westerlies. Sailboards and mountain bikes can be rented.

THINGS TO SEE & DO

Boat trips

Boats depart daily for Cape St Vincent and magnificent views of the windswept Costa Vicentina. The round trip takes approximately two hours. Fishing excursions (first-timers and experienced anglers welcome), including shark fishing, are also on offer, usually departing daily at 16.30 hours – the round trip takes approximately three hours. Catches include sea bass, bream, squid and mackerel. Ground fishing is also available if you give at least 48 hours' notice. Contact **Turinfo**
ⓣ 282 62 48 73 for details of all boat trips.

Fortaleza de Sagres

Located on the Sagres Cape that reaches out into the sea, Sagres Fortress is a National Monument today, although little remains of the original site once exploited by Prince Henry the Navigator as his school of navigation and where he also had a house. The original buildings were all but destroyed by Sir Francis Drake in the late 16th century. Parts of the fortress were rebuilt in the 18th century with cannons and batteries along the cape, warehouses and a row of houses at the southern perimeter – housing the Visitor's Centre today. There are traces of the Vila Infante (Dom Henrique's house) here, including the cistern tower, Rosa dos Ventos (Wind Rose) stone dial said to have been used as a wind compass, plus ruins of former houses and the Igreja de Nossa Senhora da Graça.
ⓣ 282 62 01 40 ⊕ 09.30–20.00 daily (May–Sept); 09.30–17.30 (Oct–Apr)

Lighthouse

Visitors may be allowed to climb the tower to inspect the twin 1,000-watt lamps, visible for up to 90 km (56 miles) and among the most powerful in Europe. Up to 200 ships navigate the busy shipping lanes every day. Opening times are at the discretion of the lighthouse keepers.
ⓐ Cabo de São Vicente

Nature and birdwatching on the Costa Vicentina

The area between Ponta de Sagres and Cabo de São Vicente is one of the most important unspoilt areas of coastline in Portugal and known as the Sagres Biogenetic Reserve. In contrast to much of the Algarve coast, there is low population density here but a rocky coastline with various habitats including marshland, cliffs, sand dunes and lagoons. Today the area is protected, and for nature lovers it is a paradise. There are around 25 species of bird nesting on the cliffs and many more migrate here during the autumn, from eagles and hawks to Egyptian vultures. The annual World Birdwatchers' Festival takes place here; for more birdwatching information contact League for the Protection of Nature (LPN) 🆆 www.lpn.pt

TAKING A BREAK

Bossa Nova ££ Friendly restaurant with terrace – serves pizza, pasta, vegetarian, meat and seafood dishes. Children's menu, too. ⓐ Rua da Mareta, Sagres ⓣ 282 62 42 19 ⓛ 12.00–24.00 daily

Pousada do Infante £££ Located in the purpose-built *pousada* (historic hotel), the restaurant has regional fish dishes. ⓐ End of N268 overlooking the fortress ⓣ 282 62 02 40 ⓛ 13.00–15.00 & 19.30–22.00 daily

AFTER DARK

Topas Disco in the centre of town playing rock and pop all night. ⓐ Near the Parque de Campismo ⓣ 916 61 03 53 ⓛ 01.00–06.00 daily

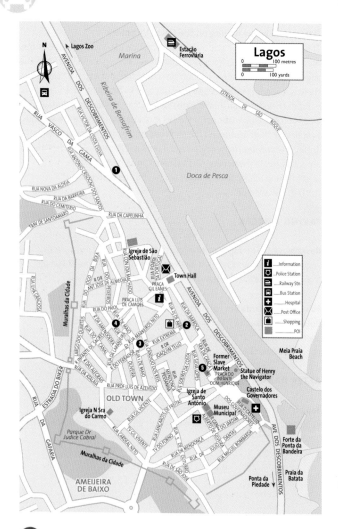

Lagos

Lagos (pronounced 'Lah-gosh') is an attractive town with a colourful past and plenty of good restaurants, shops, churches and museums.

The most famous former resident of Lagos, Prince Henry the Navigator, is commemorated by a statue in Praça do Infante Dom Henrique. In the corner of the square is an arcaded building where African slaves were once bought and sold; it is now used for art exhibitions. The massive gateway at the bottom of Rua Miguel Bombarda leads through the west side of the city walls, dating from the 14th to 16th centuries, while the rooftop of the Forte da Ponta da Bandeira (now a museum) affords excellent views of the superb natural harbour. Prettily painted houses and cobbled courtyards characterise the area around Rua da Barroca, where restaurants also cluster. Praça Gil Eanes contains a monument to King Sebastião, who was killed on an ill-fated crusading expedition to Morocco in 1578. Around the square is an extensive pedestrian precinct with bars, cafés and shops selling eye-catching local handicrafts and souvenirs. Explore the old town but don't miss the waterfront and cliff walks to the Ponta do Piedade (see page 64).

THINGS TO SEE & DO

Forte da Ponta da Bandeira (Flag Point Fort)

This tiny 17th-century fort houses some archaeological finds, a small exhibition (in Portuguese only) on the Age of Discoveries, a chapel dedicated to St Barbara and the **Taverna** restaurant.
📞 282 76 14 10 🕐 09.30–12.30 & 14.00–17.00 Tues–Sun, closed Mon
❗ Admission charge

Igreja de Santo António

The lavishly decorated 'golden' chapel is one of the few to survive the earthquake of 1755. Coloured *azulejo* tiles decorate the lower walls of the baroque chapel; the remainder is covered with fantastic ornamental woodcarving and giltwork.

🅐 Rua General Alberto de Silveira 🕐 09.00–12.30 & 14.00–17.00 Tues–Sun; closed Mon & public holidays

Lagos Zoo

Located just outside Lagos in the village of Barão de São João, Lagos Zoo has a wide selection of animals from gibbons and chimpanzees to wallabies and porcupines, plus tropical and native species of birds, tortoises, iguanas and other reptiles.

🅐 Quinta das Figueiras – Sítio do Medronhal, Barão de São João 🕐 282 68 01 00 🅦 www.zoolagos.com 🕐 10.00–19.00 (summer); 10.00–17.00 (winter)

Ponta da Piedade (Piety Point)

From Lagos waterfront you can follow the paths all the way to Ponta da Piedade, dramatic coastal rock formations with arches and stacks in the sea. You do have to be careful walking here and the flora is fragile, so boat trips are a good alternative. They leave from the Forte da Ponta da Bandeira and the Praia Dona Ana. The sunsets here are spectacular and this is also a good place for scuba diving (see page 104), dolphin-watching trips (from the marina), sailing and other watersports. Ask at the tourist office for more information.

TAKING A BREAK

On Rua Afonso de Almeida there is a row of traditional Portuguese restaurants, including Chicken Piri Piri, O Cantinho Algarvio and Pouso d'Infante. All are good, mid-priced places to sample authentic cooking.

Adega da Marina ££ ❶ Located on the waterfront, this large rustic-style restaurant is relaxed and family orientated with fresh fish and seafood from the Algarve coast. 🅐 Avenida dos Descrobrimentos 35 🕐 282 76 42 84 🅦 www.adegadamarina.com 🕐 12.00–02.00 daily

SHOPPING

Rua 25 de Abril is a small street packed with pottery shops and other crafts. Take in the *azulejos* (tiles) and wrought-iron balconies. Two of the best shops include:

Casa de Papagaio Named after its resident parrots, this is a fascinating Aladdin's cave of architectural salvage and second-hand bits and bobs. ⓐ Rua 25 de Abril

Olaria Nova Features some of the best modern pottery in the Algarve, plus traditional and ethnic clothing, shoes, accessories and jewellery. ⓐ Rua 25 de Abril

Dom Sebastião £££ ❷ Probably the town's most celebrated (and touristy) restaurant. Fish and shellfish are the specialities. Opt for a romantic evening inside rather than lunch outside. ⓐ Rua 25 de Abril 20 ⓣ 282 76 27 95 ⓛ 11.00–15.00 & 18.30–22.30 daily

Restaurante dos Artistas £££ ❸ Upmarket dining with original art on the walls and a quality international menu with dishes such as Atlantic salmon, fish ragout, vegetarian lasagne and beef stroganoff. ⓐ Rua Cândido dos Reis ⓣ 282 76 06 59 ⓛ 11.00–14.00 & 18.00–23.00 Mon–Sat, closed Sun

AFTER DARK

Bar Ferradura ❹ Excellent locals' bar run by a very friendly Portuguese owner who speaks perfect English. Cheap beer and good *petiscos* (snacks). ⓐ Rua 1 de Maio 26A ⓛ 11.00–late Mon–Sat, closed Sun

Stevie Ray's ❺ This celebrated jazz club lays on live blues and jazz on Saturday nights. ⓐ Rua de Sra da Graça 9 ⓣ 914 92 38 83 ⓦ www.stevie-rays.com ⓛ 20.30–04.00 Mon–Sat, closed Sun

Monchique

The village of Monchique (pronounced 'Mon-sheek') lies at the heart of the Serra de Monchique mountain range. Little changed by the increase of tourism, its narrow cobbled streets climb steeply, lined by traditional houses painted pastel shades of pink, blue and green, with old-fashioned gas lamps protruding here and there from the upper storeys. The Serra is also famous for its restaurants specialising in barbecue lunches of spicy chicken *piri-piri*.

THINGS TO SEE & DO

Caldas de Monchique

Caldas is famous for its hot springs, long believed to have curative and health-giving properties. It is a lovely little village lying on the edge of a densely wooded ravine, perfect for walking. The spa is still functioning, and (if you can stomach it) you can sample the original sulphurous spa water. Better known, and much more palatable, is the water bottled in the village and sold all over the Algarve. For something stronger, try *medronho*, the local liqueur made from the berries of the arbutus, or strawberry trees, that grow locally.

Walking and cycling

Outdoor enthusiasts will be in heaven in the Serra de Monchique with panoramic views of the fertile, green mountains around every bend.

FÓIA

At just over 900 m (3,000 ft), Fóia is the highest point in the Algarve. There are spectacular views of the coast, from Cape St Vincent in the west, to Vilamoura in the east. On a clear day, there are views across the rocky plateaux to terraced hillsides planted with eucalyptus, arbutus and cork oaks – sometimes even to the mountain ranges south of Lisbon.

The two highest mountains are Fóia (903 m/988 yds) and Picota (774 m/846 yds) – and it's worth visiting the villages of Alferce (for its medieval church and Roman ruins) and Marmelete (for its chapel and views). Serious walkers should get hold of a copy of the Trilhos de Bio-Park Network Monchique map. It covers 300 km (188 miles) of trails that are suitable for walking and mountain biking, all in Ordnance Survey detail.

TAKING A BREAK

Rampa £–££ Simple country restaurant with wonderful mountain views. While taking them in, tuck into the tasty, homemade soup, followed by chicken *piri-piri* (the best in town) and their delicious almond cake.
ⓐ Estrada da Fóia, Samargal ⓣ 282 91 26 20 ⓛ 11.00–late daily

Abrigo da Montanha ££ A spacious dining room in a mountain lodge, where open fireplaces add to the cosy, rustic atmosphere. The genial hosts and staff add to the experience, serving imaginative renditions of traditional Portuguese dishes. ⓐ Corte Pereiro
ⓣ 282 91 21 31 ⓦ www.abrigodamontanha.com ⓛ 19.00–22.00 daily

Bica-Boa ££ A traditional inn that has been restored by its Irish-Portuguese owners. There is a wide range of regional and international dishes on offer such as Monchique kid stew, which can be enjoyed in the dining room or on the outside terrace.
ⓐ Estrada de Lisboa ⓣ 282 91 22 71 ⓛ 10.00–24.00 daily

Jardim das Oliveiras ££–£££ A lovely restaurant in a charming rustic setting just off the main road to Fóia. Chicken *piri-piri*, snails and hearty local meat dishes are specialities. ⓐ Sitio do Porto Escuro, Monchique
ⓣ 282 91 28 74 ⓦ www.jardimdasoliveiras.com ⓛ 12.00–22.00/23.00 daily

Rouxinol ££–£££ The Scandinavian-run 'Nightingale' is set in a delightful rustic hunting lodge and offers fondues, game (in season) and a good vegetarian choice. It's also open for coffee, snacks and homemade cakes.

📍 Estrada de Monchique (opposite turning to Caldas de Monchique)
📞 282 91 39 75 🕐 12.00–21.30 (22.00 summer), closed Mon

Quinta de São Bento £££ The perfect place to celebrate a special occasion, this traditional Portuguese restaurant has won several international awards and was once the summer residence of the Portuguese Royal House of Bragança. 📍 Quinta São Bento, Estrada da Fóia (about 5 km/3 miles from town) 📞 282 91 27 00 🌐 www.restaurante-qtasaobento.site.vu 🕐 12.00–15.00 & 19.00–22.00 daily

Restaurante 1692 £££ Named after the year that the hot springs were discovered in Monchique, this restaurant serves a mixture of Algarve and Italian cuisine. On fine days you can sit outside on the Elm Tree Terrace. 📍 Caldas de Monchique 📞 282 91 09 10 🕐 12.30–22.00 daily

SHOPPING
Ardecor The place for high-quality handicrafts, clothing and accessories, wooden toys, pottery and lovely hand-painted wooden furniture. 📍 Largo dos Chorões (opposite main square), Monchique

Casa do Forno Typical Algarvian souvenirs and crafts. 📍 Rua Dr Francisco Gomes de Avelar, Monchique

Casa da Praça Some more unusual handicrafts and souvenirs, and an ideal starting point to look for that elusive gift. 📍 Praça Alexandre Herculano, Monchique

O Poço Beautiful cork ornaments; also hand-decorated pottery. The shop is on the road to Fóia. 📍 Estrada da Fóia

And... thick winter woollies may be the last thing on your mind while you are down on the sunbaked coast, but it's cool and windy at Fóia, and good-quality, hand-knitted cardigans and pullovers are always on sale here.

Portimão

A busy port on the River Arade, Portimão is also the Algarve's largest shopping centre. Wander around the town's main squares, where many of its 19th-century houses have painted tile façades and fine wrought-iron balconies, and visit some of the city's oldest sights.

THINGS TO SEE & DO

Boat trips
A half-day trip will head east past the glorious beach coves near Carvoeiro, which host a curiosity of old sea caves with dramatic arches and grottoes, and nearby towering rock formations.

Ferragudo
On the opposite side of the estuary, this quaint village has typically Portuguese architecture with a strong Moorish influence. Just beyond the village is the *fortaleza* (fortress), not open to the public, on the excellent beach of Praia Grande.

Nossa Senhora da Conçeição
It's worth going inside the Church of Nossa Senhora da Conçeição (15th–18th centuries) on the hill to take in the Gothic doorway, three naves, gilt retable and Manueline-style fonts. At the Jesuit College, which originally dates back to the 17th century, there's an original Manueline doorway and the gilt carvings and Renaissance statue inside the nave of the church.

TAKING A BREAK

The charming, flower-filled **Largo da Barca**, reached by walking underneath the arches of the Sardine Dock, is home to Portimão's best seafood restaurants, **Dona Barca** (📞 282 48 41 89) and the highly rated **Forte & Feio** (📞 282 41 88 54).

AFTER DARK

Bar Capicua Situated in the marina, this is a great place to chill out and enjoy a drink and a chat on the terrace – before hitting the dance floor. ⓐ Marina de Portimão, Bloco 4 ⓣ 282 41 12 24 ⓛ 22.00–04.00 daily

O Buque £–££ Watch the chefs transform impeccably fresh seafood into dinner in beautiful surroundings. ⓐ Parchal, 2 km (1¼ miles) from town ⓣ 282 42 46 78 ⓦ www.obuque.com ⓛ 12.00–14.30 & 19.00–22.30 Mon–Sat, closed Sun

Churrasqueira de Portimão ££ This restaurant is a typical Portuguese grill with steaks, meat and fish skewers and homemade desserts. They also deliver grilled chicken and chips in the evening. ⓐ Rua da Olivença 16 ⓣ 282 41 86 27 ⓛ 12.00–15.00 & 19.00–22.00 Mon–Sat, closed Sun

Kibom ££ A typical, one-storey Algarve house specialising in fish and shellfish. ⓐ Rua Damião L Faria e Castro ⓣ 282 41 46 23 ⓛ 11.00–15.00 & 18.00–23.00 Mon–Sat, closed Sun

Silves

This sleepy town was once the wealthy capital of a Moorish province. When the Arabs were finally expelled in 1242, the Christians returned, remodelling the castle and replacing the mosque with a cathedral. Today Silves (pronounced 'Sil-vesh') is the centre of a prosperous farming region, the pretty, unspoilt villages surrounded by orchards producing oranges, lemons, figs and other fruit in abundance.

THINGS TO SEE & DO

Arade boat trips

Take an old-fashioned Portuguese 'gondola' on a 90-minute trip to Portimão, along the River Arade, which was once the highway that brought fabulous riches to Silves.

❶ 282 42 42 43 for reservations and details **🕐** Trips Mon–Sat

Castle

This is the largest castle in the Algarve and its network of 13th-century battlements and turrets dating back to the Moorish occupation is still largely intact, though heavily restored. From the parapets the views of the Arade Valley are spectacular. In the flower-filled castle courtyard are traces of an Arab palace, built by the last Moorish ruler of Silves. The courtyard is said to be haunted by an enchanted Moorish girl. This sylph-like figure is rumoured to appear at midnight on Midsummer's Eve as she awaits the handsome prince who will one day break her spell.

🕐 09.00–18.00 daily **❶** Admission charge

Sé Velha (Old Cathedral)

Like the castle, Silves Cathedral dates from the 13th century and, despite a subsequent baroque facelift, the Gothic doorway, rib-vaulted choir and tombs of crusading knights are reminders of its medieval origins.

🕐 08.30–18.30 daily in summer; winter times vary

❶ Donation expected

Fábrica do Inglês (The Englishman's Factory)

The 19th-century English cork factory has been converted into a museum with its own brewery and six restaurants. Every night at 22.00 there is a show with singing and dancing.

ⓐ Rua Gregório Mascarenhas ⓣ 282 44 04 80 ⓦ www.fabrica-do-ingles.pt ⓛ 09.30–12.45 & 14.00–17.30 (Oct–Apr); until 22.00 May–Sept; restaurants 09.30–23.00 ❶ Admission free until 18.00

Museu Municipal de Arqueólogia (Archaeological Museum)

The museum, constructed around a 12th-century Arab well, has Bronze-Age, Roman and Moorish items.

ⓐ Rua das Portas de Loulé ⓣ 282 44 48 32 ⓛ 09.00–18.00 Mon–Sat, closed Sun ❶ Admission charge

Torreão da Porta da Cidade (Turret of the City Gate)

This barbican is the last surviving inner city wall gate. It was built in the 12th or 13th century and for many centuries was home to the municipal council. Today it holds the municipal library.

ⓛ 09.30–13.00 & 14.00–17.30 Tues–Sat, closed Sun & Mon

Alte

Alte is one of the prettiest villages in Portugal, with balconies wreathed in oleander, hibiscus and geraniums, and a striking 16th-century church. Situated 30 miles (48 km) east of Silves, it has a history stretching back to Roman times. Alte is also renowned for its singing and folk-dancing ensembles.

ⓣ 282 47 86 66 (Alte tourist office) for more details

SHOPPING

Housed in a lovely 16th-century building near the castle is the **Estúdio Destra**, the studio and gallery of Kate Swift and Roger Metcalfe, artists renowned for their hand-painted tiles and ceramics. ⓦ www.studiotiles.net

TAKING A BREAK

Casa Velha de Silves ££ Traditional Portuguese restaurant overlooking the main square, serving full meals, omelettes and sandwiches. Regular *fado* and other folk music events in the basement bar. ⓐ Rua 25 de Abril ⓣ 282 44 54 91 ⓛ 11.00–15.00 & 18.00–23.00 daily

Marisqueira Rui ££–£££ One of the finest seafood restaurants in the Algarve, with fish in tanks and crabs in their shells (they give you a mallet and a board), boiled, grilled or fried prawns, mixed seafood or meat dishes if you prefer. ⓐ Rua Comendador 27 ⓣ 282 44 26 82 ⓛ 12.00–01.00; closed Tues (in season)

Recanto dos Mouros £££ Luxury restaurant with Algarvian specialities and picturesque views of the castle. ⓐ Monte Branco ⓣ 282 44 32 40 ⓛ 12.30–15.30 & 19.00–23.00 daily

⬤ *Silves castle*

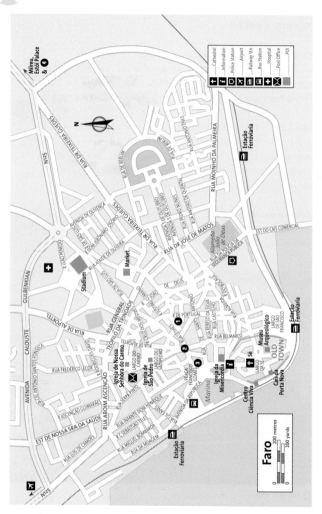

Faro

Faro

The administrative capital of the Algarve, Faro is a lively commercial centre and port with a historic Old Town with Roman wells, where you could easily spend a day sightseeing. Enter the Old Town through the Arco da Vila, an imposing Italianate gateway commissioned by the bishop of Faro after the Great Earthquake of 1755 had destroyed its medieval predecessor. Beyond the arch is the spacious central square, with its cathedral and archaeological museum and streets lined with fine houses, decorated with wrought-iron balconies. Also look out for the ancient fortifications integrated in the walls, the Corento dos Capuchos and the early-20th-century Banco de Portugal.

BEACHES

Ilha Deserta (Desert Island) is a good place to escape for the day. Catch a boat from Cais da Porta Nova between June and September. As well as a blue-flag beach there are fresh fish restaurants.

THINGS TO SEE & DO

Centro Ciência Viva (Centre of Living Science)
This is a hands-on discovery centre for children and adults.
🅐 Rua Comandante Francisco Manuel 🕒 16.00–23.00 Tues–Sun July–mid-Sept; 10.00–17.00 Tues–Fri, 15.00–19.00 Sat–Sun mid-Sept–June
❗ Admission charge

Estói Palace
This charming 19th-century palace is painted pastel pink, with bright blue *azulejo* staircases, classical statues, flower-filled urns and a riot of bougainvillaea. The building has been turned into a luxury hotel, the Pousada de Faro, but the gardens are open to the public.
🅐 Estói village 📞 289 99 40 26 🆆 www.pousadas.pt

Igreja de Nossa Senhora do Carmo (Carmelite Church)

Holds the macabre Capela dos Ossos, its walls lined with the bones of 1,200 monks. Also see the superb examples of gold-leaf carved woodwork.
ⓐ Largo do Carmo 🕒 10.00–13.00 & 15.00–17.00 daily

Milreu

These knee-high walls are all that is left of a 3rd-century AD Roman villa. The famous dolphin mosaics are still in reasonable condition.
ⓐ Signposted just before Estói 🕒 09.30–12.30 & 14.00–18.00 Tues–Sun (May–Sept); until 17.00 (winter) ❶ Admission charge

Museu Arqueológico (Archaeological Museum)

Housed in a 16th-century convent, the 1894 Archaeological Museum is the Algarve's oldest museum. Highlights include a beautiful 3rd-century AD Roman mosaic of Neptune surrounded by the four winds and a section dedicated to the Moorish occupation.
ⓐ Praça Afonso III, Old Town ❶ 289 89 74 04 🕒 10.00–18.00 Tues–Fri, 10.30–17.00 Sat–Sun (Oct–Apr); 10.00–19.00 Tues–Fri, 11.30–18.00 Sat–Sun (May–Sept) ❶ Admission charge

Sé (Cathedral)

Climb the tower (68 steps) in this 13th-century building near the Archaeological Museum to enjoy great views over the town and lagoon.
ⓐ Old Town, Largo da Sé 🕒 Consult tourist office for current opening hours. Church open Sun only during services ❶ Admission charge

TAKING A BREAK

Restaurante Gengibre e Canela £ ❶ This vegetarian restaurant has a lunch buffet service and à la carte dinner. Expect veggie lasagne, quiches and fruit salads. ⓐ Travessa da Mota 10 ❶ 289 88 24 24 🕒 12.00–15.00 Mon–Sat, closed Sun

Adega Dois Irmãos ££ ❷ Since 1925 the 'Two Brothers' have been satisfying the palates of visitors and locals with superb fish and seafood. Atmospheric traditional tiled dining room. ⓐ Praça Ferreira de Almeida 25 ❶ 289 82 33 37 ⓒ 12.00–23.00 daily

Café Aliança ££ ❸ This traditional Portuguese café is one of the oldest in the country, dating back to 1905. Patrons have included prime ministers as well as the French writer Simone de Beauvoir, and Portugal's favourite modernist poet, Fernando Pessoa. ⓐ Praça Francisco Gomes ❶ 289 80 16 21 ⓒ 08.00–22.00 daily

The Old Coach House Restaurant £££ ❹ Fine dining restaurant in the stunning country-house hotel of Monte do Casal on the way to Estói Palace. The menu is mainly modern cuisine with French-based specialities. Pricey but you can try the 'taster' menu with five small gourmet courses. ⓐ Cerro do Lobo, Estói ❶ 289 99 15 03 ⓦ www.montedocasal.pt ⓒ 12.30–14.30 & 19.00–21.30 daily

🔺 *A quiet backstreet in Faro Old Town*

Tavira & Cabanas

Tavira is an elegant town and nicely complements the growing resort of Cabanas. The coast here fragments into a series of spits, lagoons and barrier islands, which together constitute the Ria Formosa nature reserve. The warm waters on the shore side of the sandbanks are perfect for swimming, while the Atlantic beaches provide just the right conditions for windsurfing.

Get your bearings in Tavira by climbing the cobblestone lanes leading off Rua da Liberdade to the ruined **castle** (🕐 09.00–17.00). From the little garden within the walls there are good views of the estuary and town, and it's possible to count some of the domes and spires of Tavira's 22 churches. Next to the castle is the **Igreja de Santa Maria do Castelo** (the Church of St Mary of the Castle), built on the site of a former mosque, and remarkable for its double bell tower and enormous clock.

Also see the church of Nossa Senhora das Ordas for its decorative ceilings and the medieval town hall.

BEACHES

Tavira beach can be reached by ferry from the Quatro Aguas jetty between May and October. Other beaches nearby include **Pedras da Rainha,** which has its own offshore sandbank, reached by boat or on foot at low tide, and **Santa Luzia,** from where there is a footbridge to Tavira Island. There is also a small railway from Pedras d'el Rei, near Santa Luzia, to **Praia de Barril** and the extensive beaches of Tavira Island.

THINGS TO SEE & DO

Ria Formosa Natural Park

A beautifully wild area of salt marshes and lagoons, this reserve embraces some of the best beaches in the region. Ria Formosa is also the breeding ground of many species of wading bird.

The **Visitors' Centre** (📍 Quinta de Marim (1 km/¹/₂ mile) from Olhão on EN125 🕐 09.00–12.30 & 14.00–17.00) provides a good introduction to the area. **Ilha Deserta** (📞 917 77 91 55 🌐 www.ilha-deserta.com) and **Sequa Tours** (🌐 www.sequatours.com) offer guided tours of the lagoons by boat, a great way to spot the wildlife.

Tourist train

A tourist train departs from Pedras da Rainha resort to the attractive fishing village of **Cabanas de Tavira** from June–Oct from 09.00–19.00.

🔺 *Salt marshes of Ria Formosa Natural Park*

TAKING A BREAK

Cabanas

Restaurant Pizzeria Fenícia £ Located in the centre of Tavira and boasting a good choice of toppings, this pizza restaurant is a good option for a quick eat for all the family. ⓐ Largo da Caracolina ⓣ 281 32 51 75 ⓛ 12.00–14.30 & 19.00–22.00 Mon–Sat, closed Sun

Pedros £–££ Typical Portuguese restaurant, specialising in razor clams with beans, monkfish, *cataplana* and seafood rice. ⓐ Rua Capitão Batista Marçal 51 ⓣ 281 37 04 25 ⓛ 12.30–15.00 & 18.00–22.00 Tues–Sun, closed Mon

Restaurante Baixamar £–££ Facing the Ria Formosa, specialities at this restaurant include the fish soup, squid and tuna steaks. ⓐ Avenida Engenheiro Duarte Pacheco ⓣ 281 38 11 84 ⓛ 12.00–14.30 & 19.00–22.30 Tues–Sun, 12.00–16.30 Sun

Dona Inês ££ Large family-friendly restaurant with an attractive terrace for alfresco dining. ⓐ On the Cabanas–Tavira road ⓣ 281 37 08 01 ⓛ 12.30–15.00 & 18.30–22.30 Tues–Sun, closed Mon

Piano Bar ££ Popular seafront restaurant serving English and international dishes. Children's menu and off-road patio. ⓐ Avenida 28 Maio 2 ⓛ 18.30–late Mon–Sat, closed Sun

Restaurante Ideal ££ Family restaurant with a wide range of Portuguese cuisine from fish skewers to steaks and with a terrace in warm weather. ⓐ Rua Infante Dom Henrique 15 ⓣ 281 37 02 32 ⓛ 12.00–15.00 & 19.00–22.00 Thur–Tues, closed Mon

Tavira

Imperial £–££ An award-winning Portuguese restaurant. Try the *serra bucho de marisco* (mixed seafood with pork). ⓐ Rua José Pires Padinha 22 ⓣ 281 32 23 06 ⓛ 12.00–22.00 daily

Beira Rio ££ On the river, by the old bridge, this restaurant has a good selection of vegetarian dishes. Meat eaters should try the baked turkey.
ⓐ Rua Borda d'Agua da Assecia 46–52 ⓣ 281 32 31 65 ⓛ 19.00–23.00 daily

O Canecão ££ 'The world's best *cataplana*' is the boast at this shellfish specialist restaurant. ⓐ Rua José Pires Padinha 162 ⓣ 281 32 62 78
ⓛ 12.00–15.00 & 18.00–24.00 Fri–Wed, closed Thur

Kudissanga ££ A fascinating menu of dishes from the old Portuguese colonies. ⓐ Rua Dr Agusto Silva Carvalho 8 ⓣ 281 321 670 ⓛ 12.00–02.00 Fri–Mon & Wed, 19.00–02.00 Thur; closed Tues

O Patio ££–£££ Highly regarded rooftop restaurant, with an international menu and Portuguese specialities. ⓐ Rua Dr António Cabreira 30
ⓣ 281 32 30 08 ⓛ 11.00–15.00 & 18.00–24.00 Mon–Sat, closed Sun

Quatro Águas £££ Highly rated, smart, traditional fish and shellfish restaurant near the quay by the beach. ⓐ Quatro Aguas ⓣ 281 32 53 29
ⓛ 12.00–15.30 & 18.30–22.30 daily

AFTER DARK

Arco Bar Lively bar popular with the gay crowd. Has good music, cocktails and food. Can be quite pricey, though.
ⓐ Rua Almirante Cândido dos Reis 67 ⓣ 281 32 35 37 ⓛ 18.00–02.00 daily

Discoteca Ubi & Bubi Bar One of Tavira's veteran nightlife hangouts, this bar is located in a former jam factory. ⓐ Antiga Fábrica Balsense, Rua Almirante Cândido dos Reis ⓛ Discoteca Ubi 01.00–10.00 Aug–Sept; Oct–July Sat only; Bubi Bar 21.00–04.00 all year

Skipper's Tavern This English-style pub has live music on Thursdays. They also have food, wi-fi and show sports on a big screen. ⓐ Avenida Dr Mateus Teixeira de Azevedo (near train station) ⓣ 281 32 89 08

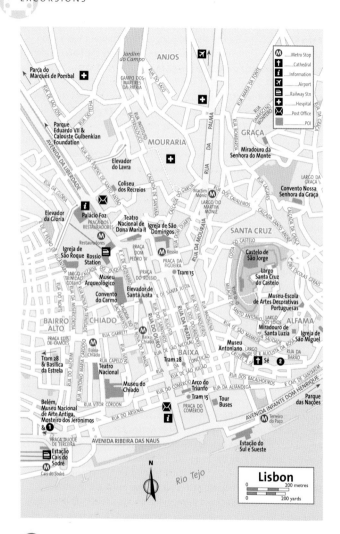

Lisbon

Ⓜ	Metro Stop
✝	Cathedral
ℹ	Information
✈	Airport
🚆	Railway Stn
✚	Hospital
✉	Post Office
	POI

0 — 200 metres
0 — 200 yards

Lisbon

One of the great historic capitals of Europe, Lisbon is also a port with an exciting, cosmopolitan atmosphere. Built on a series of hills at the estuary of the Rio Tejo (River Tagus), its many attractions include **Castelo de São Jorge** (St George's Castle), the **Belém Tower** and the **Mosteiro dos Jerónimos** (Jeronimos Monastery), the medieval Alfama quarter and the restaurants and *fado* clubs of the Bairro Alto.

It is possible to see quite a few of Lisbon's top attractions in a short time if you plan well. Start at the **Praça do Comércio** on the riverfront. The main tourist office is here, where you can buy **Lisboa Cards** (1, 2 or 3-day card with free or discounted entrance for many attractions plus public bus, trams, lifts and metro) and catch hop-on, hop-off sightseeing tour buses. You can also take tram 15 to **Belém**, which is by far the best way to get to the **Museu Nacional de Arte Antiga** (alight at Santos), one of the country's best museums.

At the northern end of Praça do Comércio you'll see the **Arco do Triunfo**, an elaborate archway topped with figurines representing glory and valour, as well as explorer Vasco da Gama and the Marquês de Pombal (who rebuilt the city after the devastating earthquake of 1755). The archway leads to the grid-like **Baixa** – a vibrant shopping area dominated by the central pedestrian street of **Rua Augusta**. From Rua da Conceição, which crosses it, you can take tram 28 east to the **Alfama** to visit the **Sé** (cathedral), the **Castelo de São Jorge** and take in the fabulous city views from the **Miradouro de Santa Luzia**. Take the tram westwards to reach the **Chiado, Bairro Alto** and **Estrela**, with its iconic white-domed Basilica. This tram is a quick and easy way to see the historic quarters of the city, but watch your wallet as it's renowned for pickpockets preying on tourists. You can also take the **Elevador de Santa Justa** (Rua de Santa Justa) to the Chiado/Bairro Alto. This iron lift is similar to the styles used in Paris at the time of Gustave Eiffel. There's a café at the top, or alight for the **Convento do Carmo**, a majestic ruin that stands as a homage to the earthquake and is worth a visit.

At the top end of the Baixa are **Praça do Rossio** and the adjacent **Praça da Figueira**, two vibrant squares filled with cafés. At the northern end of Rossio you'll see the **Teatro Nacional de Dona Maria II** – if you have time go to the 'hole-in-the-wall' bar in the small square to the right and try some *ginjinha* cherry liqueur before seeking out Rua das Portas de Santo Antão, a street of restaurants behind the theatre. To the left of the theatre is the neo-Manueline **Rossio Station**. The road this side leads onto **Praça dos Restauradores**, dedicated to the restoration of power to the Spanish in 1640, and on to the **Avenida da Liberdade**, a tree-lined avenue modelled on the Champs Elysées in Paris. You'll find designer stores and large hotels along here, and at the top end is **Parque Eduardo VII**, a large park with formal gardens, hothouses with tropical plants plus more views over the city. The **Calouste Gulbenkian Foundation** (with its two art museums, orchestra and choir, this is the most important cultural organisation in the country) lies just northwest of here (metro Praça de Espanha). You can either walk or take the metro from Pombal back to Baixa-Chiado.

If you have time, take a metro to the **Parque das Nações** (Nations' Park), a modern district built for Expo '98, the beautiful town of **Sintra** (a UNESCO World Heritage Site with castles and palaces surrounded by lush parkland) and the nearby resort towns of **Cascais** and **Estoril**.

🔺 *Castelo de São Jorge, Lisbon*

THINGS TO SEE & DO

Castelo de São Jorge (St George's Castle) Alight from tram 12 or 28, or bus 37, walk uphill, then follow the castle walls to the entrance. Originally built in the 5th century by the Visigoths and fortified by the Moors, the castle has seen several reconstructions and destruction by earthquakes. As you enter the Praça das Armas (square), look out for the statue of Dom Afonso Henriques, Portugal's first king, and take in the city views. Walk round the castle to climb the battlements and towers, relax in the café and look out for the resident peacocks.
ⓐ Alfama ☎ 218 80 06 20 🕐 09.00–sunset

Mosteiro dos Jerónimos Built by the king Dom Manuel I, this is one of the greatest national monuments in Portugal, a UNESCO Heritage Site, and a testament to the elaborate Manueline architecture. See its regal, religious, seafaring and naturalistic symbols on the portals and inside the Church of Santa Maria, plus the tranquil cloisters and *azulejo* tiles in the former refectory.
ⓐ Praço do Império ☎ 213 62 00 34 🌐 www.mosteirodosjeronimos.pt
🕐 10.00–17.00 Tues–Sun (18.00 in summer), closed Mon. The **Archaeological Museum** is next door and on the riverfront you shouldn't

SHOPPING

The famous flea market (**Feira da Ladra** – literally, 'Thieves' Fair') opens early on Saturday and Tuesday around **Campo de Santa Clara** in the picturesque **Alfama** district. In the **Baixa** there's traditional street shopping with international chains as well as local leather and jewellery stores. The **Armazens do Chiado** has several floors of fashion and household stores – take the exit at the Chiado for designer shopping and individual boutiques or head up to the **Avenida da Liberdade**. For everything in one place, visit one of the city's large indoor shopping centres – the **Colombo**, **Amoreiras** or the newest place, **Vasco da Gama**, in Parque das Nações.

miss the **Torre de Belém**, a fortress-tower in the river with more examples of Manueline architecture, and the **Padrão dos Descobrimentos**, a monument dedicated to the Golden Age of Discovery.

Sé (Lisbon Cathedral) Founded in 1150 to celebrate the re-taking of the city from the Moors by Dom Afonso Henriques, this is an imposing Romanesque building with twin crenellated towers, giving it a fortress-like appearance. It's free to get in but worth paying to see the Gothic cloisters built by King Dinis in the 14th century.
ⓐ Largo da Sé ⓛ 09.00–19.00 daily

TAKING A BREAK

Try the art nouveau cafés on Lisbon's main boulevard, **Avenida da Liberdade**, between **Rossío Dom Pedro IV** and **Praça do Marquês de Pombal**. For a more 'old world' atmosphere, head for **Alfama**, where the tiny, unpretentious restaurants specialise in fish. In the evenings, the action traditionally moves to **Bairro Alto**, a lively neighbourhood of densely packed, 17th-century houses with small, reasonably priced restaurants.

Antiga Confeitaria de Belém £ ❶ No trip to Lisbon is complete without a visit to its most famous café – try the *pastéis de Belém* (custard tarts) hot from the oven and admire the elaborate tiled walls.
ⓐ Rua de Belém 84–92 ⓣ 213 63 74 23 ⓛ 08.00–23.00 daily
(Sun until 22.00)

AFTER DARK

Clube de Fado ❷ Another must in Lisbon is a visit to a *fado* restaurant. There are several in the Bairro Alto but this one in the Alfama is one of the best. There's typical Portuguese cuisine here and, although pricey, it's worth it for the quality and the entertainment by live *fado* singers nightly. ⓐ Rua S João da Praça ⓣ 218 85 27 04 ⓦ www.clube-de-fado.com
ⓛ 20.00–02.00 daily ❗ Reservations required

Loulé

A busy little town, famous for its gypsy market, Loulé (pronounced 'Loo-lay') is also a flourishing centre of local handicrafts and one of the best places in the region to see artisans at work. Be sure to walk among the ruins of its 13th-century Arab castle or visit the adjacent 17th-century church.

THINGS TO SEE & DO

Igreja de Nossa Senhora da Conceição

Across the street from the castle is this attractive 17th-century church. The walls are decorated with blue-and-white tiles depicting scenes from the life of the Virgin.

ⓐ Rua Paio Perez Correia ⏱ 10.00–12.00 Mon–Fri, 10.00–14.00 Sat, closed Sun

Loulé Castle

Only the walls remain of Loulé's Arab fortress, rebuilt in the 13th century. Climb the stone steps to the battlements and three towers for fine views of the town and the surrounding countryside.

ⓐ Largo da Matriz ⏱ 09.00–17.30 Mon–Thur, 10.00–14.00 Sat, closed Sun

SHOPPING

There's a **daily market** in Loulé, in the Moorish-style building at the top of the main street, the Avenida José da Costa Mealha, but most visitors come on Saturday morning to see the colourful **gypsy market**. There's no shortage of gifts and souvenirs – everything from handbags and *esparto* (sea grass) mats to painted roosters and ceramic plates, as well as an enormous range of food, including olives, spices, cheeses and jars of local honey.

Museu Municipal de Arqueologia

Next door to the tourist office, housed in the commander's residence in the old castle, is a small exhibition of Roman coins and pottery and a reconstruction of a traditional Algarvian kitchen.

ⓐ Edifício do Castelo ⓛ 09.00–17.30 Mon–Fri, 10.00–14.00 Sat, closed Sun

TAKING A BREAK

Restaurante Moinho Ti Casinha £ This popular restaurant next to a watermill in a village north of Loulé has rustic Algarvian dishes such as baked bacalhau (dried and salted cod) and pork with plums. ⓐ Ribeira das Mercês, Querença ⓣ 289 43 81 08 ⓛ 12.30–13.30 & 19.30–21.30 Mon–Sat, closed Sun

A Muralha ££ Tucked under the castle walls, serving *cataplana*, hot-stone steaks and fresh fish kebabs, this is one of the town's oldest restaurants. The garden is sweet with jasmine. ⓐ Rua Martin Moniz 41 ⓣ 289 41 26 29 ⓛ 12.00–15,00 & 19.00–23.00 Tues–Sat, closed Sun & Mon

Avenida Velha ££–£££ Long-established, well-known Portuguese restaurant specialising in fresh fish dishes from the Algarve and Alentejo. ⓐ Avenida José da Costa Mealha 40/Rua Rainha D Leonor ⓣ 289 41 64 74 ⓛ 12.00–15.30 & 18.00–22.30 Mon–Sat, closed Sun

A Quinta ££–£££ On the old Loulé road from Almancil, this stylish restaurant with an international menu has lovely views over the coast. Try stewed mussels with coriander and wine. ⓐ Rua Vale Formosa ⓣ 289 39 33 57 ⓛ 12.00–14.30 & 19.00–22.00 daily (Mar–Nov)

Bica Velha £££ Highly rated Portuguese and international cooking served up in the oldest building in town. ⓐ Rua Martim Moniz 17/19 ⓣ 289 46 33 76 ⓛ 18.00–24.00 Mon–Sat, closed Sun ⓘ Reservations recommended

---

▶ *António Chainho is a famous Portuguese* fado *guitarist*

LIFESTYLE
The Portuguese way

Food & drink

SOUPS & STARTERS

Usually made from fish or vegetables, soups make a nourishing, tasty and relatively cheap option for a first course. Try *caldo verde*, made from shredded cabbage and potatoes, often served with thin slices of sausage, or *caldeirada de peixe*, a delicious fish soup similar to a *bouillabaisse*. Cured ham and shellfish are good alternatives.

BACALHAU À ALGARVIA

Salt cod fish is a Portuguese favourite – the Algarvian style is fried and served with potatoes, onion and garlic.

CATAPLANA

This tasty seafood casserole takes its name from the wok-like copper vessel the food is cooked in. Apart from clams, the ingredients usually include prawns, mussels and pieces of white fish steamed in their own juices. Pork and/or spicy sausage is often added. Servings of *cataplana* are usually for a minimum of two persons.

FRESH FISH

A typically Algarvian dish, charcoal-grilled sardines are cheap and available everywhere, always served with fresh bread and boiled potatoes. The daily catch in most resorts includes tuna, swordfish, sea bass, bream, sole and red mullet. Most types of fish are simply grilled, but tuna is often cooked in a delicious casserole with onions and peppers.

MEAT DISHES

Popular with tourists, chicken *piri-piri* is an African-influenced dish in which the chicken pieces are brushed with a chilli and olive oil sauce before being grilled. Steak or pork fillets are usually served in generous portions. *Bife à Portuguesa*, sirloin steak cooked with smoked ham and potatoes in the oven, is a succulent national dish. Also look out for *caldeirada de cabrita*, an appetising lamb or kid stew.

◆ *Typical restaurant in the Algarve*

DESSERTS

Save room for one of the delicious Portuguese desserts, choosing from crème caramel, chocolate mousse, rice pudding, almond tart or *queijo de figo* (layers of dried figs, ground almonds, cinnamon and chocolate).

DRINKS
Soft drinks

Citrus fruits are plentiful in the Algarve, though freshly squeezed juice is surprisingly expensive. The tap water is drinkable, but it is less palatable than the home-produced mineral water from Monchique.

Port

Portugal is, of course, the origin of this famous fortified wine. The name comes from the city of Oporto, where much of it was made in the 17th century. Brandy was added to stop fermentation during the voyage. Apart from the more common ruby, tawny and late bottled vintage port varieties, you'll come across a dry white port, served chilled as a delicious aperitif.

Wine

Portugal is a major wine-producing country, and a bottle of wine with a meal won't break the bank. Most restaurants will have an acceptable *vinho da casa* (house wine). If you want red, ask for *vinho vermelho*, if white, *vinho branco*. *Vinho verde* (literally, 'green wine') is actually a youthful and slightly sparkling wine, well suited to seafood.

COFFEE

The Portuguese are great coffee drinkers and there are numerous ways it can be served:

- espresso-style black coffee is *um café* or *uma bica*.
- coffee with milk is *café com leite*.
- iced coffee is *café gelado*.
- regular black coffee is *uma carioca*.

CHECKING THE BILL

In Portuguese restaurants, there is a small cover charge for bread and butter, which comes with olives, fish spread and cheese. If you don't want these, say so. The Portuguese equivalent of VAT (called IVA) is usually added automatically to the bill and amounts to 12 per cent of the total. Tipping is at your own discretion, but 10 per cent would be appreciated.

Wine produced locally in the Algarve (look for the Lagoa label) tends to be high in alcohol and a little on the rough side. Portugal's better vintages are grown further north. They include Dão (similar to a Burgundy) and two good-value wines from the Alentejo region, Borba and Redondo.

Beer and spirits

Sagres and *Super Bock*, two good-quality lagers, are the most popular Portuguese brands. The local firewater, *medronho*, is distilled from the fruit of the arbutus tree. *Brandymel*, made with Portuguese brandy and locally produced honey, is a sweet liqueur, like the delicious almond-based *amêndoa amarga*.

● *Grilled sardines are cheap and available anywhere*

Menu decoder

MENU ITEMS & COOKING TERMS

On Portuguese menus, the dishes are often described very simply, with the main ingredient and the cooking method, as in *coelho assado* (roast rabbit). Here is a list of the most common ingredients and cooking methods.

GENERAL TERMS

Gelado Ice cream

Molho Sauce

Prato de dia Dish of the day

Sobremesa Dessert

INGREDIENTS

Alho Garlic

Almôndegas Meatballs

Ameijoas Clams

Arroz Rice

Atum Tuna

Azeitonas Olives

Besugo Bream

Bife (*also* **vaca**) Beef

Bolo Cake

Borrego Lamb

Caracóis Snails

Cavala Mackerel

Cebola Onions

Chouriço Spicy sausage

Coelho Rabbit

Costeletas Chops

Favas Broad beans

Feijóes Beans

Frango Chicken

Gambas Prawns

Lagostins Lobster

Limão Lemon

Linguado Sole

Lulas Squid

Manteiga Butter

Mariscos Shellfish

Pão Bread

Peixe Fish

Pescada Hake

Pimenta Pepper

Polvos Octopus

Porco Pork

Presunto Cured ham

Queijo Cheese

Robalo Sea bass

Sal Salt

Salsichão Salami

Truta Trout

Vitela Veal

Vinagre Vinegar

COOKING METHODS

Assado Roast

Cozido Boiled

Estufado Stewed

Fumado Smoked

Grelhado Grilled

Guisado Stewed

Nas brasas Braised

No forno Baked

Água (fresca) Water (iced)

Bica Espresso-style coffee

TYPICAL PORTUGUESE DISHES

Bacalhau Salt cod, cooked numerous ways, often with olives, garlic, onions and hard-boiled egg

Bife de cebolada Steak braised in wine and onions

Caldeirada Fish soup with onions and potatoes

Caldo verde Soup of mashed potato and shredded cabbage

Cataplana Seafood casserole

Cozida portuguesa A rich casserole of beef, pork, sausages, rice and vegetables

Sopa de grão Chickpea, tomato and onion soup

Sopa de marisco Seafood soup

DRINKS

Cerveja Beer

Chá Tea

Galão White coffee (served in a tall glass)

Gelo Ice

Vinho (branco/vermelho) Wine (white/red)

Vinho de mesa/vinho da casa Table wine/house wine

Shopping

MARKETS

Every town of any size in the Algarve has a permanent covered market
where local people shop (in preference to the supermarket) for
inexpensive fruit, vegetables and fish. Larger markets also have stalls
selling bread, cured ham and local cheeses. Street markets are colourful
affairs and you may pick up some bargains – ceramics, wicker baskets,
lacework, linen, even old liquor stills. If you don't like the price, it's
acceptable to barter.

Market days at a glance

This listing shows the day or days of the month on which you will find
markets in towns along the Algarve coast.

- Albufeira – 1st and 3rd Tues
- Almancil – every Sun
- Alvor – 2nd Tues
- Faro – 2nd Sun
- Lagos – 1st Sat
- Loulé – 2nd Sat
- Portimão – 1st Mon
- Quarteira – every Wed
- Sagres – 1st Fri
- Silves – 3rd Mon
- Tavira – 3rd Sat & 3rd Sun

BASKETRY

Basket weavers still work out of doors in the summer months. One
popular spot to catch them practising their skills is on the EN125 near
Boliqueime (for Loulé).

CERAMICS, TILES & POTTERY

Among the most popular items are painted *gallos* (cockerels), inspired by
a Portuguese folk tale. You'll also find miniature chimneys and brightly
coloured jars and vases. *Azulejo* tiles – of the kind found in churches and
other historical buildings – are only expensive if genuinely old. They are
sold singly or in sets.

The best-known potteries in the Algarve are at Porches, 3 km
(1.8 miles) east of Lagoa, where the speciality is floral-patterned *majolica*.

⬥ *Pottery is a popular choice of souvenir*

Visit **Artesanato Reis** (🕐 Mon–Sat 09.00–20.00 in summer) in Porches, where you can see the craftsmen hand-painting flowers, birds, fish and other motifs.

Other pottery outlets are:

- **Artesanato Regional Casa Matias** Traditional pottery. ⓐ Mercado Municipal, Tavira 🕐 Closed Sun
- **Casa Algarve** Sells locally produced pottery, old and new. ⓐ Alqueives, Porches
- **Infante Dom Henrique** Earthenware pottery. ⓐ Rua Candido dos Reis, Albufeira
- **Olaria Algarve** Watch the craftsmen at work at this Porches outlet. ⓐ Alqueives, Porches 🕐 Mon–Fri all day & Sat mornings

COPPER & BRONZE

Bowls, trays, scales, small stills and lamps are often made locally. The **Caldeiraria Louletana** (Rua da Barbacã, Loulé) is a workshop specialising in handmade brass and copperware.

CORK

Portugal is the world's largest exporter, and is famed for its cork products, ranging from placemats to whole sculptures. **O Poco**, Estrada da Foia, Monchique, sells a variety of cork items.

HANDICRAFTS

Throughout the Algarve, shops specialising in *artesanato* sell products such as baskets, cork mats, lace tablecloths, woollen shawls, handmade rugs, brightly painted earthenware jars, copper lamps, confectionery, cockerels and *caravelles* (traditional sailing vessels made from wood).

General arts and crafts outlets:
Alexandre Herculano ⓐ Monchique ⓛ Daily
Alquatro ⓐ Estrada de Vale do Lobo, Almancil ⓛ 10.00–13.00 & 14.00–19.00 Mon–Fri, closed Sat & Sun
Aquário ⓐ Praça da República, Portimão ⓛ Daily
Arisol ⓐ Alporchinhos, Porches ⓛ Mon–Sat, closed Sun
Bazar Tânger ⓐ Rua José Pires Padinha, Tavira ⓛ Mon–Sat, closed Sun
Centro de Artesanato Rugs, ceramics, straw dolls, cork placemats, palm-leaf items, lace shawls, caravelles. ⓐ Loulé ⓛ Daily
Estabelecimentos Sol Dourado ⓐ Rua Dr Teófilo Braga, Vila Real de Santo António ⓛ Mon–Fri & Sat mornings, closed Sun
João Calado Earthenware Cast iron, pottery, glazed tiles, cork and sconces. ⓐ Torre, Lagos ⓛ Daily
Porta da Moura ⓐ Rua do Repouso, Faro ⓛ 10.00–20.00 daily

JEWELLERY, GOLD & SILVERWARE

Portuguese craftsmen are famous for filigree – fine threads of gold or silver delicately interwoven to produce brooches and pendants, resembling birds, flowers or cockerels. *Marcasite*, a grey-black metallic mineral, was used in Moorish jewellery and is inexpensive.

For original jewellery:
Allerbon ⓐ Marina, Vilamoura

Ingrid Serrão ⓐ Rua Direita, Portimão
Mogodor ⓐ Rua Gil Eanes, Lagos

LEATHERWARE

Handbags, belts (often ornamented), wallets, purses, shoes and boots are all excellent value in Portugal, and generally of excellent quality. In Rua da Barbacã, in Loulé, you can shop for leather belts and other items; at the same time you can watch the local artisans at work, making saddles and harnesses.

MUSIC

Take home a recording of *fado* music (see page 9) as a memento of your visit. Artists to look out for include Amália Rodrigues, Carlos do Carmo, Madredeus and Mariza.

WINES & SPIRITS

Any large supermarket will have a large selection of wines and spirits. The best Algarvian wines carry the Lagoa label. Also look out for Borba, Redondo, Dão, the light wine known as *vinho verde* and quality wines from the Douro region. Port is widely available, either well-known British brands like Croft and Cockburn or Portuguese labels, including Ferreira. Wine shops also stock varieties of *medronho* (arbutus-berry liqueur). Alternatively, take home some of the delicious sweet liqueur made from almonds, known as *amêndoa amarga*, or *brandymel*, Portuguese brandy blended with honey. As there are now restrictions with hand luggage it might be better to buy wines and drink at the airport unless the merchant can arrange direct shipment.

Faro airport's departure lounge has a shopping arcade and is good for any last-minute purchases before you head home. Here you can snap up handicrafts, drinks, tobacco, perfumes, regional sweets, cheeses, coffee, tea, delicatessen products, cameras, leather goods, books, stationery and CDs. 🕔 07.00–24.00 daily

Children

CHILDREN'S ACTIVITIES

The Algarve is a great holiday destination for families. Children are cherished in Portugal and you will find they are welcome in most restaurants. There is sometimes even a separate children's menu available. Most tour operators offer a kids' club in the larger hotels, providing appropriate activities for different age groups throughout your stay. This provides them with supervision and friends away from their parents if they choose the activities on offer. A lot of hotels offer a baby-sitting service as well. In addition to this, there are a number of activities in the Algarve aimed at children.

The beautifully clean beaches of the Algarve are ideally suited to young families. You can rent pedalos at most resorts. In particular, the lakes at Quinta do Lago make a very safe environment for pedalos, rowing boats, canoes, etc. There is even a children's playground here.

Conditions at Praia da Rocha and Lagos are ideal for children learning to windsurf. **The Windsurf Centre** at Meia Praia, Lagos, runs 'Kids Days' (age 9–16 years only). The programme includes windsurfing lessons, volleyball, beach games and lunch – all under the watchful eye of a lifeguard. 🕐 10.30–16.00 Mon & Fri, closed Sat & Sun, June–Sept
📞 282 79 23 15

BOAT TRIPS

Day excursions on the water leave from most resorts. Boats explore the grottoes, as well as offering opportunities for swimming, diving and snorkelling. While older children will relish the adventure, be aware that younger children may get bored. It may also be a good idea to take a boat trip on your second week, when the children have acclimatised a little to the sun and heat.

FAMILY RESTAURANTS

Most restaurants in the Algarve welcome children. Some even have high-chairs and children's choices on the menu.

KRAZY WORLD

Inland from Albufeira, this fun park, set in scenic surroundings, is well worth the half-hour trip. The attractions include crazy golf, a mini-zoo, crocodile shows, swimming pools, a Quad circuit and pedalos on the lake, plus bar, pizzeria and souvenir shop. ⓐ Algoz ⓣ 282 57 41 34 ⓦ www.krazyworld.com ⓛ 10.00–18.00 Wed–Sun (Oct–June); 10.00–19.30 daily (July–Aug)

PICNICS

Picnics are worth considering if you're planning a drive, a day out in the countryside or want to avoid pricey snack bars at tourist sites. There are fully stocked supermarkets in all Portuguese resorts, but remember that most shops close for lunch (usually ⓛ 13.00–15.00). The local market is a much more interesting place to shop – here you will find the freshest fruit and vegetables (especially oranges, peaches and figs), as well as assorted local breads, sausages, cheeses and hams.

WATER PARKS

Ideal for children of all ages (and adults too!), it is possible to spend a whole day in one of the Algarve's water parks. The biggest and best is

🔺 Family water fun at Algarve's water parks

Slide & Splash. Aqua Show may be a quieter day for young families. Each has a number of amazingly convoluted slides, as well as junior pools, snack bars and other amenities. Fully qualified lifeguards are always on hand. Private buses take customers to and from the resorts.

Slide & Splash ⓐ Vale de Deus, Estombar, near Armação de Pêra (see page 31)

Aqua Show ⓐ Semino Quarteira (see page 42)

Aqualand ⓐ Alcantarilha (see page 27)

ZOOMARINE

This spectacular attraction features dolphin, sea-lion and seal shows. Other amenities include aquariums, swimming pools, a cinema and a funfair. ⓐ On the EN125 at Guia, near Albufeira ⓣ 289 56 03 00 ⓦ www.zoomarine.com (see page 36)

⬥ *A seal performing for the crowd at Zoomarine*

Sports & activities

BIRDWATCHING
Local birdwatching trips can be organised through the tourist offices in Portimão and Lagos (see page 15 for details).

CYCLING
Bicycles and motorbikes can be rented out by the day from **Motorent** at the following main resorts:
Lagos ❶ 282 76 97 16
Praia do Carvoeiro ❶ 282 35 65 51
Praia da Rocha ⓐ Hotel Rocha 2 ❶ 282 41 69 98

FISHING
Centro de Pesca da Quinta do Lago Fishing on the salt-water lake. Prices include all fishing equipment (see the tourist office for details and bookings) ⓐ Av 5 de Outubro 18, Faro ❶ 289 80 04 00
Cepemar Big-game fishing for hammerhead shark, marlin, swordfish, bonito and 200 other species. ⓐ Portimão ❶ 282 04 14 76

HORSE RIDING
The following centres offer excursions and riding lessons for all ages, as well as refreshments and other facilities.
Centro Hípico ⓐ Vilamoura ❶ 289 30 25 77/916 71 89 29
Grande Vale de Ferro Riding ⓐ Mexilhoeira ❶ 282 96 84 44
ⓦ www.horseridingholiday.eu
Horse Shoe Ranch ⓐ Mexilhoeira ❶ 289 47 13 04
Pinetrees ⓐ Almancil ❶ 289 39 44 89
Quinta dos Amigos ⓐ Quarteira ❶ 289 39 33 99
Quinta Martins ⓐ Almancil ❶ 289 39 55 29
Tiffany's Riding Centre ⓐ Lagos ❶ 282 69 73 95
ⓦ www.teamtiffanys.com
Vale Navio ⓐ Albufeira ❶ 289 54 28 70
Also see ⓦ www.equisport.pt for countywide centres.

SCUBA DIVING
Blue Ocean Divers ⓐ Lagos ⓣ 964 66 56 67
Divers Cove ⓐ Carvoeiro ⓣ 282 35 65 94
Indigo Divers ⓐ Albufeira ⓣ 289 58 70 13
Tivoli Dive Centre ⓐ Lagoa ⓣ 282 35 19 94

SPORT & FITNESS CENTRES
Barringtons Squash courts, gymnasium, cricket pitch with nets, snooker room, sauna and Turkish bath, indoor and outdoor swimming pools and, for golfers, putting green, pitching green, driving range and tuition option. Daily and weekly membership available. ⓐ Vale do Lobo ⓣ 289 35 19 40 ⓦ www.barringtons.pt

Brown's Tennis and squash courts, gymnasium, indoor and outdoor swimming pools, snooker tables, table tennis and darts. ⓐ Vilamoura ⓣ 289 32 27 40 ⓦ www.browns-club.com

Burgau Sports Centre Tennis and squash courts, sauna, gymnasium, pool, table tennis, many other sports, swimming pool and children's playground. ⓐ Burgau ⓣ 282 69 73 50

TENNIS
Racket hire as well as tuition are available at the following centres.
Brown's (see above)
Burgau Sports Centre (see above)
Performance Tennis School ⓐ Lagoa ⓣ 282 35 78 47
Rocha Brava Tennis Club ⓐ Carvoeiro ⓣ 282 35 78 47
Vale do Lobo Tennis Academy ⓐ Vale do Lobo ⓣ 289 35 78 50

WALKING
Portugal Walks Organises day and half-day walks. ⓣ 292 69 72 98 ⓦ www.portugalwalks.com

Festivals & events

Algarve Guide – a brochure published in several languages by the regional tourist authority gives up-to-date listings of cultural events. Also see Ⓦ www.algarve.pt

January
1–6 January Carol singing in the local villages.

February
Carnival all over the Algarve in the weekend prior to Shrove Tuesday.
Loulé Carnival The biggest and best, with bands, floats and dancers.

March
20 March Alvor holds its annual *feria* (festival) with entertainment including live music and traditional *fado* performances.

April
Throughout the Algarve there are religious processions in the lead-up to Easter, especially on Palm Sunday and Good Friday.

May
1 May The May Day folk festival involves traditional singing and folk dancing – celebrated in Alcoutim, Albufeira, Alte, Monchique.
International Film Festival ❶ 282 42 26 67 Ⓦ www.algarvefilmfest.com

June
International Music Festival The biggest event of its kind in the Algarve, with performances by world-famous artists.
Festival Med World music festival in Loulé Ⓦ www.festivalmed.com.pt
Tavira 'Saints Festivities' Processions and street decoration. ❶ 281 32 25 11

July
Algarve Jazz Festival International and local musicians in Loulé.

Feira do Carmo Handicrafts festival in Faro.
Faro Motorbike Festival Bike convention and rock music.
Silves Beer Festival Local Portuguese beers, with tastings, in the grounds of the castle, plus brass band concerts and folk dancing.

August

29 August Banho de 29 in Lagos – fireworks and live music on the local beaches.
Festival do Marisco Seafood festival in Olhão.
Folk dancing Shows and concerts of *fado*, folk and classical music are held in the Tavira gardens all through the summer. ❶ 281 32 25 11
Lagoa 'Fatacil' country fair Handicrafts, tourism, agriculture, commerce and local industry, with live bands, craft exhibitions, food and wine tasting, shows, exhibitions and competitions.
Medieval Festival at Castro Marim in Silves.

September

Algarve Photo Salon in Silves.
Lagoa Wine Festival Tastings to promote the local varieties and vintages.
Monte Gordo 'Nossa Senhora das Dores' annual fair With games, side shows, folk concerts and other musical entertainment. After Monte Gordo the fair moves on to Tavira.
National Folklore Festival A showcase for traditional Portuguese folk music and dancing. Various venues, culminating in the final competition at Praia da Rocha.

October

Choirs Festival Concerts from all over the Algarve.
Monchique Country Fair Exhibition of local handicrafts.

December

8 December Ceremonial blessing of the crib in many churches.

❶ *Main roads are rarely busy in the Algarve*

PRACTICAL INFORMATION
Tips & advice

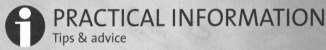

Accommodation

Price ratings are based on a double room for one night.
£ = up to €75   **££** = €75–£150   **£££** = over €150

Club Praia da Rocha £–££ Giant hotel complex with more than 1,300 apartments of various sizes, swimming pool, kids' pool, restaurants and just five minutes' walk from the beach. ⓐ Avenida Comunidade Lusiada, Praia da Rocha Ⓦ www.alpharooms.com

Hotel Carvoeiro Sol ££ Located on Carvoeiro's village square, just metres from the beach, this is a small hotel (54 rooms), with simply styled rooms, a pool, terrace and bar. ⓐ Praia do Carvoeiro Ⓣ 282 35 73 01 Ⓦ www.carvoeirosol.com

Hotel Salema ££ Small hotel overlooking the beach in Salema. Most rooms have balconies, plus there's a breakfast room and bar. ⓐ Rua 28 de Janeiro, Praia de Salema Ⓣ 282 69 53 28 Ⓦ www.hotelsalema.com

Hotel Montechoro ££–£££ One of the newest hotels in the Albufeira area, there are 322 air-conditioned rooms here, two outdoor pools, two restaurants, rooftop bar, piano bar, summer barbecues, tennis courts and golf nearby. ⓐ Rua Alexandre O'Neill, Albufeira Ⓣ 289 58 94 23 Ⓦ www.hotelmontechoro.pt

Pousada de Sagres ££–£££ Located in the village of Sagres and built in a traditional Portuguese style with whitewashed walls and red-tiled roof, this upmarket hotel looks over the Atlantic Ocean. There's a restaurant and bar at the hotel along with a tennis court and swimming pool. ⓐ Ponta da Atalaia, Sagres Ⓣ 282 62 02 40 Ⓦ www.pousadas.pt

Monchique Spa Resort £££ Set in the heart of the Monchique mountains, this spa resort is a relaxing hideaway with various packages and accommodation, including hotels, apartments and an inn in the historic centre and the Thermal Baths Hotel, which has a spa onsite. The Spa includes a restaurant (see page 68), gym, a pool with massaging jets and bubbles, whirlpool, shower, sauna and steam room, massages and beauty treatments. ⓐ Caldas de Monchique ❶ 282 91 09 10 ⓦ www.monchiquetermas.com

Pestana Alvor Praia £££ 5-star hotel located on the beach west of Portimão with contemporary air-conditioned rooms, restaurants and bars, indoor and outdoor salt-water pools, health club and gym, tennis courts, driving range and putting green, plus several golf courses nearby. ⓐ Praia Tres Irmãos, Alvor ❶ 282 40 09 00 ⓦ www.pestana.com

Tivoli Marina £££ 5-star hotel with a prime position overlooking Vilamoura Marina, but with its own landscaped gardens, private beach, pools, restaurants and bars, plus year-round entertainment. ⓐ Vilamoura Marina ❶ 289 30 33 03 ⓦ www.tivolimarinotel.com

Vila Valverde £££ Originally built in the 19th century, this manor house has been converted into a modern country hotel. Located 25 minutes (on foot) from the beach, it has contemporary, stylish rooms, all with balconies, ample grounds with lawns and orange trees, both indoor and outdoor pools plus a small fitness centre. ⓐ Estrada da Praia da Luz ❶ 282 79 07 90 ⓦ www.vilavalverde.com

Vila Vita Parc £££ Set in extensive landscaped grounds, this five-star resort has tastefully incorporated Moorish-style architecture in its public areas, rooms and apartments. Along with a golf course, pitch and putt and putting green, there are tennis courts, a wellness centre, kids' activities, tours and nearby watersports concessions and easy access to the beach. ⓐ Alporcinhos, Porches ❶ 282 31 01 00 ⓦ www.vilavitahotels.com

Preparing to go

GETTING THERE

By air

The cheapest way to get to the Algarve is to book a package holiday with one of the leading tour operators. Operators specialising in the Algarve offer flight-only deals or combined flight-and-accommodation packages at prices that are hard to beat by booking direct. If your travelling times are flexible, and if you can avoid the school holidays, you can find some very cheap last-minute deals using websites. You should also check the travel supplements of weekend newspapers, such as *The Sunday Times* or the *Sunday Telegraph*. They often carry advertisements for inexpensive flights, as well as classified listings for privately owned villas and apartments to rent in the Algarve.

Charter flights can be subject to long delays, so if time is critical, you might be better off paying more to travel by scheduled flight. The Portuguese national carrier, **TAP**, offers daily flights to the Algarve, operating from Heathrow. Some flights are direct, while others involve a change in Lisbon. TAP's UK office ❸ Gillingham House, 38–44 Gillingham Street, London SW1V 1HU ❶ 0845 601 0932 Ⓦ www.flytap.com. **British Airways** also offers charter flights (❶ 0844 493 0787 Ⓦ www.britishairways.com), as does the no-frills airline **easyJet** (Ⓦ www.easyjet.com); and **Ryanair** flights from Dublin have regular connections from various UK airports (Ⓦ www.ryanair.com).

Many people are aware that air travel emits CO_2, which contributes to climate change. You may be interested in the possibility of lessening the environmental impact of your flight through the charity Climate Care, which offsets your CO_2 by funding environmental projects around the world. Visit Ⓦ www.jpmorganclimatecare.com

By rail

Travelling to the Algarve from the UK takes 2–3 days, but might be an option if you're buying a multi-country train pass with stops along the way. From London St Pancras you can travel by Eurostar to Paris's Gare du Nord

Station, then transfer to Paris Montparnasse and take a train to Irún (Gipuzkoa in Basque) in the Basque Country (Spain), and change again for a train to Lisbon. For further information about booking contact Rail Europe on ☎ 08448 484 064 or see Ⓦ www.raileurope.co.uk. If you're flying to Porto or Lisbon, then taking the train can be a cheaper way of reaching the Algarve than flying. The fastest trains are Comboios and slightly slower Intercidades, which operate between Porto Campanhã and Lisbon Oriente (and Santa Apolonia) and from Oriente to Faro. You can book tickets online at Ⓦ www.cp.pt and it's worth paying the little extra for first class.

TOURISM AUTHORITY

The UK branch of the Portuguese National Tourist Office is located at the Portuguese Embassy in 11 Belgrave Square, London SW1 8PP. They have a brochure line ☎ 0845 355 1212 or you can browse online at Ⓦ www.visitportugal.com. You can also find UK tour operators that specialise in Algarve holidays and accommodation online at Ⓦ www.portugaloffice.org.uk. The regional Algarve tourist office website is Ⓦ www.visitalgarve.pt and there are offices at Faro Airport and in all the main resorts and towns mentioned in this book.

BEFORE YOU LEAVE

Holidays should be about fun and relaxation, so avoid last-minute panics and stress by making your preparations well in advance.

It is not necessary to have inoculations to travel in Europe, but you should make sure you and your family are up to date with the basics, such as tetanus. It is a good idea to pack a small first-aid kit to carry with you, containing plasters, antiseptic cream, travel-sickness pills, insect repellent, bite relief cream, antihistamine tablets, painkillers and remedies for upset stomachs.

Sun lotion can be more expensive in the Algarve than in the UK, so it is worth taking a good supply of high-factor lotions. If you are taking prescription medicines, ensure that you take enough for the duration of your visit – you may find it impossible to obtain the same medicines in the Algarve. It is also worth having a dental check-up before you go.

ENTRY FORMALITIES

If you're travelling from EU countries, you can enter Portugal with either a valid passport or identity card. Citizens from Canada, the USA, Australia and New Zealand must have a valid passport but don't need a visa unless they are staying for longer than 90 days. Those from South Africa do need a visa.

MONEY

In line with the majority of EU member states, Portugal entered the single currency on 1 January 2002. Euro (€) note denominations are 500, 200, 100, 50, 20, 10 and 5. Coins are €1 and €2, and 1, 2, 5, 10, 20 and 50 céntimos.

You will need some currency before you go, especially if your flight gets you to your destination at the weekend or late in the day after the banks have closed. Traveller's cheques are a safe way to carry money, because the money will be refunded if the cheques are lost or stolen; however, they can be difficult to cash in Portugal. ATMs are also safe and give a good exchange rate. Make sure you take a little money with you in case you arrive at a weekend or late in the day when the banks and bureaux are closed. Some UK banks require up to a week's notice to order currency and traveller's cheques but there are bureaux de change at UK airports. While traveller's cheques are a safe way to carry money, it can be difficult to find somewhere to cash them and cash is often preferred in rural areas.

If you plan to use credit, charge or debit cards while you are away, call your bank or card company before you leave to let them know where you are going. Otherwise you may find your card abruptly stopped while you are away. You can also check that your cards are up to date – you do not want them to expire mid-holiday – and that your credit limit is sufficient for those holiday purchases. Don't forget, too, to check your PINs in case you haven't used them for a while – you may want to draw money from cash dispensers while you are away.

Banks Open Monday to Friday 08.30–15.00. There are exchange shops (câmbios) everywhere in the Algarve. You will need to show your passport when exchanging traveller's cheques.

Credit cards These are widely accepted at garages, shops and restaurants in the major towns, but cash is preferred in more rural areas.

CLIMATE

The weather in the Algarve has attracted tourists to the region for centuries, and the climate is one of the most settled in the world. With over 3,000 hours of sunshine a year, the climate is similar to that of northern Africa. Winters are generally mild, with temperatures rarely dipping below 10°C (50°F); summers are hot, often exceeding 30°C (86°F). A constant feature of the annual climate is the sea breeze, refreshing in summer, bracing in winter. Rainfall is low and falls mostly in October and November, and February and March.

BAGGAGE ALLOWANCE

Tightening of airport security has meant that baggage allowances are restricted for all passengers passing through the UK. Each passenger is allowed one item of cabin baggage through the airport search point measuring a maximum of 56 cm x 45 cm x 25 cm (22 x 18 x 10 inches). Handbags and other bags should be placed inside this one item.

It's better to place all liquid items, including water, other drinks, sprays, creams, pastes and gels, in your hold baggage if possible. If you really want to take liquids, gels and aerosols in your cabin baggage, you must place them in individual containers of 100 ml and carry them in a transparent, re-sealable bag no bigger than 20 cm x 20 cm (8 x 8 inches). For updates and more details on transport security, please see
Ⓦ www.dft.gov.uk

During your stay

AIRPORTS

The main airport for the Algarve is at Faro, and this is one of the cheapest and most competitive routes in Europe, thanks to the sheer number of charter flights travelling between the UK and the Algarve. Even so, flights are often fully booked during the peak holiday periods, including Christmas: the Algarve is a very popular winter-sun destination.

If you land by day from the south, you will have a stunning view of the Ria Formosa Nature Reserve, where land and sea meet in a protected zone. The airport has many of the services you would expect, including a bank, a post office, a tourist office, shops and restaurants. Faro is the capital of the Algarve region and therefore all transport services are available, including car rental. Faro Airport (FAO) is located on the western side of Faro city in the Central Algarve so is equidistant to either end of the region.

Car hire

Several car-hire companies operate at Faro Airport, including: **Alamo** (Ⓦ www.alamo.co.uk), **Autojardim** (Ⓦ www.autojardim.com), **Avis** (Ⓦ www.avis.co.uk), **Europcar** (Ⓦ www.europcar.com), **National** (Ⓦ www.nationalcar.com), **Rentauto** (Ⓦ www.rentauto.pt) and **Sixt** (Ⓦ www.sixt.co.uk). Alternatively, see **Holiday Autos** (Ⓦ www.holidayautos.co.uk) to search for the best deals.

GETTING TO AND FROM THE AIRPORT
By car

If you are driving, you should leave the airport via the N125-10, then follow signs for the N125 (EN125) towards Olhão, Tavira and Vila Real de Santo António if you're heading east, or the IC4 then N125 towards Almancil and Vilamoura if heading west. If you're going further than this, you should stay on the IC4 and then take the motorway east or west towards your destination.

BEACH SAFETY

Take note of the flag system that advises you of swimming conditions.

- **Green** = safe bathing and swimming for all
- **Yellow** = caution – strong swimmers only
- **Red** = danger – no swimming

By bus

The airport bus runs to Faro city centre at regular intervals from outside the arrivals terminal. The first and last buses from the airport are at 07.10 and 21.17 and the journey takes about 20 minutes. From Faro city centre there are several buses running to destinations throughout the Algarve – see ⓦ www.eva-bus.com for more details.

By taxi

Taxis leave from outside the arrivals hall and run on a meter, but as a rule charge around €1 per km. The taxis are only allowed to take four passengers plus luggage and charge a surcharge between the hours of 21.00 and 06.00. You can obtain an instant quote for your taxi online at ⓦ www.faroairportguide.com/taxis.htm or look at the table of approximate fares.

BEACHES

In summer, many beaches have lifeguards and a flag safety system. Other beaches may be safe for swimming, but there are unlikely to be life-saving amenities available. Bear in mind that the strong winds that develop in the hotter months can quickly change a safe beach into a not-so-safe one, and some have strong currents the further out you go. If in doubt, ask the tourist office or at your hotel.

● *Beautiful beaches in the Algarve*

COMMUNICATIONS

If you wish to use your **mobile phone** on holiday, check with your phone company before you leave to find out if your mobile will work in Portugal and how much the calls will cost you. The main networks in Portugal are Vodafone, Optimus and TMN.

Public telephones in Portugal are either coin or card operated. Card-operated phones take credit cards or telephone cards, which can be purchased in many *tabacarias* (newsagents/cigarette shops).

Postal service

Post offices are known as *correios* and are open on weekdays between 08.30 and 18.00 hours. There are often bigger post offices in the larger towns, which may also open on Saturday mornings. Second-class post is posted in the red post boxes. First-class post, known as *correio azul* (blue post), goes in the blue post boxes. You will sometimes see international post boxes as well. There are generally two collections a day – one at 13.00 and one at 18.00 hours.

TELEPHONING PORTUGAL

To call Portugal from overseas dial the international dialling code (UK, Ireland, New Zealand and South Africa = **00**, Australia = **0011** and USA = **011**) followed by 351 then the three-digit area code and the six-digit number.

TELEPHONING ABROAD

To call an overseas number dial 00 followed by the country code (UK = **44**, Ireland = **353**, Australia = **61**, New Zealand = **64**, South Africa = **27**, USA = **1**).

CUSTOMS

The Portuguese are a gentle and friendly people. A simple good morning (*bom dia*) or good afternoon (*boa tarde*) will delight them. The sense of the family is very strong; the early evening walkabout and family churchgoing are still popular. Children are welcome in most places, and you'll get used to seeing them out late in restaurants.

Contrary to popular opinion, the Portuguese do not take a *siesta*, but they do close for between one and three hours for lunch. The larger shopping centres do not close at all.

When dining at a restaurant don't be surprised if you're given cutlery with fruit. The Portuguese can deftly skin and eat a banana with a knife and fork, but as a foreigner you're let off some of the cultural norms.

ELECTRICITY

Portugal uses the standard round-pin European plug. It is a 220-volt system as opposed to the 240-volt UK system. Before you buy electrical appliances to take home, always check they will work in the UK.

EMERGENCIES
Hospitals
Hospital Particular do Algarve Morada: Estrada de Alvor Lote 27, Cruz Bota-Alvor, 8500-322 Portimão ❶ 282 42 04 00 Ⓦ www.hpalg.com

Faro District Hospital ❸ Rua Leão Penedo, 800-385 Faro ❶ 289 89 11 00

Lagos District Hospital ❸ Rua Castelo dos Governadores
❶ 282 77 01 00

Portimão – Barlavento Hospital ❶ 282 45 03 30

Dr Bernard Landau Medical and dental clinic, 24-hr emergency service, home visits ❸ Oura Village, Av Infante D Henrique, Areias S João, 8200-261 Albufeira ❶ 289 58 89 23 (24 hrs) ❸ ihclda@mail.telepac.pt

Dr Jan van Dijk, GP 24-hr emergency service ❸ Rua das Acacias 9, Areias S João, 8200-277 Albufeira ❶ 289 54 20 61 ❸ vandijk@mail.telepac.pt

Embassies
British Embassy ❸ Rua de São Bernardo 33, 1249-082 Lisbon
❶ 213 92 40 00 Ⓦ http://ukinportugal.fco.gov.uk/eng

British Consulate ❸ Apartado 609, Edificio a Fabrica, Avenida Guanaré, 8501-915 Portimão ❶ 282 49 07 50

US Embassy ⓐ Avenida das Forças Armadas, 1600–081 Lisbon
ⓣ 217 27 33 00 ⓦ http://portugal.usembassy.gov
Canadian Embassy ⓐ Avenida da Liberdade 198–200, 3rd Floor, 1269–121
Lisbon ⓣ 213 16 46 00
Australian Embassy in Portugal ⓐ Avenida da Liberdade 200,
2nd Floor, 1250-147 Lisbon ⓣ 213 10 15 00
ⓦ www.portugal.embassy.gov.au

EMERGENCY NUMBERS

- Dial **112** – the operator will put you through to **police**, **fire brigade** or **ambulance**.
- Report any theft or accident to the police and your holiday representative or the hotel staff, who also keep a list of English-speaking doctors and local pharmacies.

GETTING AROUND
Driving

To rent a car in Portugal you must be over 21 years old and have held your licence for at least one year. You will need to show your driving licence and carry it with you whenever you are driving (as will any other named drivers on your rental agreement). Make sure the insurance cover is sufficient for your needs.

Driving in Portugal can be unpredictable, so take extreme care. Drivers here can be impatient when faced with a driver who is not used to the area. Many back roads are very narrow and the surfaces may be uneven. However, a lot of main roads have recently been resurfaced, and motorways are being extended for easier access to all parts of Portugal.

Taxis

Taxis can be hired from railway stations, bus stations and taxi ranks. If you decide to use a taxi for a longer journey (a day trip, for example), it is

RULES OF THE ROAD

- Always carry your driving licence, car-rental papers and passport. Police checks are infrequent, but you will be fined if you do not have the correct papers.
- Seat belts are compulsory, even for back-seat passengers. Children under 12 are not allowed in the front.
- The speed limit is 120 kmh (74 mph) on motorways, 90 kmh (56 mph) on highways, and 40–50 kmh (25–30 mph) in villages, towns and cities.
- Drink-drive and speeding laws are rigorously applied. The alcohol limit is lower than in the UK, the blood alcohol level is not allowed to exceed 0.05%.
- Local driving can be erratic and road surfaces poor. Always drive with extreme caution.

possible to negotiate the fare. It will help to write down your destination – many drivers speak only limited English.

Buses

Buses operate along the main EN125 highway, linking the resorts and main villages. Stops are marked with blue-and-white *paragem* signs. Timetables are posted at stops. Tickets for local buses are sold on board by the driver. Enquire about passes, which are sold at bus terminals or ticket agencies. Express buses operate between the main towns. Tickets for these must be bought from a bus terminal or ticket agency before boarding. It is advisable to book in advance at the height of the season.

Trains

A railway runs from Vila Real de Santo António near the Spanish border to Lagos in the west. If you are not in a hurry, this is a good way to see inland Algarve. The trains are clean and airy, if a little basic, and very cheap. Be warned that a number of stations – Loulé, Silves and Albufeira, for example – are some distance from the town centres.

HEALTH, SAFETY & CRIME

Pickpockets are common in crowded areas, especially outside monuments and at markets. Be particularly wary of people asking you the time, as they are probably trying to distract you while someone else attempts to snatch your bag or wallet. Use traveller's cheques or credit cards rather than cash and carry a photocopy of your passport, leaving the original in the hotel safe. In the event of being robbed or attacked, try to report the incident to the police (*poner una denuncia*) as soon as possible (at least within 24 hours). This is extremely important if you wish to obtain a statement (*denuncia*) to make an insurance claim. If reporting the loss or theft of your passport, you will also need to get in touch with the British Consulate, who can arrange a new passport (time permitting) or issue a temporary document to get you home. It is a good idea to take photocopies of your passport before leaving home, and to keep these in a separate place from your other documents.

The abundance of street-life means that you will rarely find yourself alone or in a position to be harassed. However, women may be intimidated by men passing comment as they walk by, or even following them. This pastime, known as *piropo*, is common throughout the Latin world and is not meant as a threat.

Health

The biggest danger you are likely to face is overexposure to the sun, particularly from May to October when temperatures can reach up to 45°C (113°F). Try to avoid walking in the midday sun and stay in the shade whenever possible. Drink plenty of bottled mineral water. It is advisable to wear sunglasses and a hat when you are out sightseeing.

It is a good idea to stick to bottled water at all times, especially in the summer when the river beds dry up and cause pollutants in the water system to become concentrated. Food in Portugal is as reliable as anywhere else in Europe, but be wise about where you eat and contact a doctor if you think you have food poisoning.

Health insurance

Public hospitals in Portugal can provide you with emergency treatment – the old E111 forms are now invalid but EU citizens should apply for a European Health Insurance Card (EHIC), which entitles you to reduced-cost and sometimes free medical treatment. You can apply for this online from the UK Department of Health (W www.ehic.org.uk) or by calling ☎ 0845 605 0707. You should also take out your own travel insurance. This is not just to cover the loss of your luggage or personal belongings while away, but also against any unforeseen medical emergency and repatriation costs.

Police

There are three types of police service in Portugal.

Polícia Municipal Local police

Polícia de Segurança Pública (PSP) National police in blue uniform

Guarda Nacional Republicana (GNR) Militarised police in green uniform

MEDIA

There are a few English-languagenewspapers published in Portugal, including the *APN* (Anglo-Portuguese News) and the *Portugal News*, plus the *Algarve Resident*. The online *Algarve Observer* (W www.algarveobserver.com) is also worth a look. They provide stories about national news and events within the English communities. They also give a timetable of cinema showings and theatre events. Many UK newspapers are available in Portugal. You can often buy them on the day of issue, due to the fact that they are printed simultaneously in Spain and the UK.

OPENING HOURS

Shops ⏱ 09.00–19.00 with a break for lunch between 12.00 and 15.00. New shopping centres often have longer hours, 10.00–23.00, including Sundays, with no lunch break.

Museums ⏱ 10.00–17.00, again with a break for lunch. Many museums are closed on Mondays as well as public holidays.

Banks ⏱ 08.30–15.00 Mon–Fri

Pharmacies 🕐 09.00–19.00, with a break for lunch. A sign in the window will tell you which pharmacy is open until 22.00 hours and where the all-night pharmacy is.

RELIGION

Portugal is predominantly Roman Catholic, with church services held most evenings and every Sunday. Many saints' days are celebrated, often as public holidays, so some tourist sights will be closed and churches may have extra services. However, you may be lucky enough to join in the raucous celebrations at a festival to commemorate a saint's day.

SMOKING

Smoking is banned in most enclosed public spaces. Hotels are permitted to allocate smoking floors and rooms.

TIME DIFFERENCES

Portugal follows Greenwich Mean Time (GMT). During Daylight Saving Time (late Mar–late Sept), the clocks are put forward by one hour. In the Portuguese summer, at 12.00, the time in Australia, New Zealand, South Africa, UK and USA is as follows:

Australia: Eastern Standard Time 21.00, Central Standard Time 20.30, Western Standard Time 19.00

New Zealand: 23.00

South Africa: 13.00

UK: 12.00

USA: Eastern Time 07.00, Central Time 06.00, Mountain Time 05.00, Pacific Time 04.00, Alaska 03.00

TIPPING

In general, the Portuguese will only leave a couple of euros for a large meal. However, in the Algarve where there are lots of tourists, it has become quite normal to tip 10 per cent. It's not that normal to tip taxi drivers but in the more upmarket restaurants and hotels, a tip might be the norm and even expected. Don't feel under pressure, though.

TOILETS

Public toilets are few and far between, and not the most savoury of
places when they do exist. The best place to find toilets is at any of the
larger shopping centres, where they're generally clean and modern.
Failing this you might have to use one in a nearby café or restaurant, but
you will have to buy something.

TRAVELLERS WITH DISABILITIES

Despite EU regulations facilities for wheelchair users are very poor in
the Algarve and many of the ramps and kerbs designed for wheelchairs
are still inadequate. Better facilities can be found in the international-
standard hotels, where foreign travel agencies have insisted on
them. The situation is improving and most municipal areas will have
reasonable facilities. Bus stops have been adapted to enable easier
access and there are designated disabled places available on buses.
Many streets are cobbled, and there are often steep hills or steps. This
makes it difficult to gain access to a number of places.

🔺 *Traditional door*

ACKNOWLEDGEMENTS

We would like to thank all the photographers, picture libraries and organisations for the loan of the photographs reproduced in this book, to whom copyright in the photographs belongs: Algarve Tourist Board pages 7, 9, 124; Bigstockphoto 77; Flickr.com/Rui Ornelas page 79; Hotel Montechoro page 54; Pictures Colour Library pages 5, 10, 30, 107, 116; Rogers Associates page 84; Thomas Cook pages 13, 15, 21, 27, 30, 38, 46, 58, 73, 97, 101, 102; Turismo de Portugal pages 73, 91 (Antonio Sacchetti); Wikimedia Commons page 89; World Pictures/Photoshot pages 18, 43, 53

Project editor: Tom Willsher
Layout: Donna Pedley
Proofreader: Nick Newton
Indexer: Marie Lorimer

Send your thoughts to
books@thomascook.com

- Found a beach bar, peaceful stretch of sand or must-see sight that we don't feature?

- Like to tip us off about any information that needs a little updating?

- Want to tell us what you love about this handy, little guidebook and more importantly how we can make it even handier?

Then here's your chance to tell all! Send us ideas, discoveries and recommendations today and then look out for your valuable input in the next edition of this title.

Email to the above address or write to:
pocket guides Series Editor, Thomas Cook Publishing, PO Box 227, Coningsby Road, Peterborough PE3 8SB, UK.

Useful phrases

English	Portuguese	Approx pronunciation
BASICS		
Yes	Sim	*Seem*
No	Não	*Nown*
Please	Por favor	*Poor favohr*
Thank you	Obrigado/a	*Ohbreegahdoo/a*
Hello	Olá	*Ohlah*
Goodbye	Adeus	*Adayoosh*
Excuse me	Com licença	*Cong lisensah*
Sorry	Desculpe	*Dishkoolper*
That's okay	Está bem	*Istah bayn*
I don't speak	Não sei falar	*Nown say falahr*
Portuguese	Português	*Portoogehsh*
Do you speak English?	Fala Inglês?	*Fahla eenglaysh?*
Good morning	Bom día	*Bohm deea*
Good afternoon	Boa tarde	*Boha tahrd*
Good evening	Boa noite	*Boha noyt*
My name is ...	Chamo-me ...	*Shamoo-mi ...*
NUMBERS		
One	Um	*Oong*
Two	Dois	*Doysh*
Three	Três	*Traysh*
Four	Quatro	*Kwahtroo*
Five	Cinco	*Seengkoo*
Six	Seis	*Saysh*
Seven	Sete	*Set*
Eight	Oito	*Oytoo*
Nine	Nove	*Nov*
Ten	Dez	*Desh*
Twenty	Vinte	*Veengt*
Fifty	Cinquenta	*Seengkwayngta*
One hundred	Cem	*Sayng*
SIGNS & NOTICES		
Airport	Aeroporto	*Aehrohportoo*
Railway station/	Estação de Caminho	*Ishtasowng di kamihnyo di*
Platform	de Ferro/Linha	*fehrroo/Leenya*
Smoking/	Fumadores/	*Foomadohrsh/*
non-smoking	Não fumadores	*Nown-foomadohrsh*
Toilets	Lavabos	*Lavahboosh*
Ladies/Gentlemen	Senhoras/Homens	*Sinyohrash/Omayngsh*